Yoga of S<

"This exciting and liberating book opens with an otherworldly experience involving the late-night intersection of deeply emotional music of jazz saxophonist John Coltrane with an apparition of multiple-witnessed unexplained aerial phenomena above New York City in 1976. Grosso describes his own awakening to the universal and idealistic origins of music, especially of a deeply transcendental nature, through his years of training under Swami Nada Brahmananda (whose name literally means Divine Music Happiness), against the lovely background of cosmic humor and deep wisdom imparted by such an enlightened soul. His sage observations and recollections are a gift to the world, hungry as it is for deeper meaning and purpose accessible to the individual seeker. Music is philosophy—this book is a joy!"

EBEN ALEXANDER, M.D., AUTHOR OF PROOF OF HEAVEN

"Michael Grosso has done it again. After his monumental work on the levitating Saint Joseph of Cupertino, who defied the laws of physics with his literal flights of devotion, rising tens of feet into the air, he now brings us images of a modern mystic, Swami Nada Brahmananda, via the ecstatic and transcendental music of the spheres. Part memoir, part biography of the twentieth century ascetic Swami Nada Brahmananda, Grosso's new work offers a rich vision into a magical world of mysticism, intertwined with his own mystical experiences and tempered by his keen analytic attention to detail."

LORILIAI BIERNACKI, PH.D., PROFESSOR OF RELIGIOUS STUDIES
AT THE UNIVERSITY OF COLORADO AT BOULDER

"Reading this book was for me a wonderfully joyous experience, something to treasure, especially at the present time of 'Kali Yuga,' the age of conflict. The story of Michael Grosso's encounter with his one-time music teacher Nada Brahmananda—and his rare type of ancient music yoga—is a colourful tapestry of philosophy, extraordinary experiences, and everyday life in 1970s New York, woven together by the spell of music seen as a spiritual practice. In this context, 'learning by heart' needs to be taken literally, meaning a great deal more than memorizing: it is a route to transcending one's everyday self, to expanding awareness to encompass the 'unstruck' sound, the unheard melody of the universe. This is indeed a book for music lovers everywhere and also for all those who enjoy exploring different ways of acquiring wisdom and reconnecting with living nature."

ZOFIA WEAVER, AUTHOR OF *OTHER REALITIES?:*
THE ENIGMA OF FRANEK KLUSKI'S MEDIUMSHIP

"Michael Grosso introduces us to one of the most remarkable men of our time, Swami Nada Brahmananda, who lived in perfect health to the age of 97, rarely needing to sleep for more than an hour or two, who didn't dream (confirmed by scientists), and who, apparently, didn't have much use for thinking (it makes one dull, he said). This swami, shunning honors or fame, lived to teach others, including the author, the transcendental power of music and made his own body itself a musical instrument and a channel through which the divine could sing. *Yoga of Sound* is itself a remarkable book and deserves to be included among such classics as *Autobiography of a Yogi,* Ram Dass's *Be Here Now,* and the books of Carlos Castañeda. In short, stunning, mind-blowing, and a marvel of the miraculous."

KENNETH RING, PH.D., AUTHOR OF *LESSONS FROM THE LIGHT*

"Why do so many people take music either *too* seriously or not nearly seriously enough? *Yoga of Sound* conveys an essential truth: pure music is *life,* lived to the fullest, and *that* suggests divinity: unlimited and unknown powers. This book may help us understand why George Harrison was fond of the saying: *God likes me when I pray, but loves me when I sing.*"

TOBIAS CHURTON, AUTHOR OF
THE SPIRITUAL MEANING OF THE SIXTIES

Yoga of Sound

The Life and Teachings of the Celestial Songman, Swami Nada Brahmananda

A Sacred Planet Book

MICHAEL GROSSO

Inner Traditions
Rochester, Vermont

Inner Traditions
One Park Street
Rochester, Vermont 05767
www.InnerTraditions.com

Text stock is SFI certified

Sacred Planet Books are curated by Richard Grossinger, Inner Traditions editorial
board member and cofounder and former publisher of North Atlantic Books. The
Sacred Planet collection, published under the umbrella of the Inner Traditions family
of imprints, includes works on the themes of consciousness, cosmology, alternative
medicine, dreams, climate, permaculture, alchemy, shamanic studies, oracles,
astrology, crystals, hyperobjects, locutions, and subtle bodies.

Cataloging-in-Publication Data for this title is available from the Library of Congress

ISBN 978-1-64411-637-1 (print)
ISBN 978-1-64411-638-8 (ebook)

Printed and bound in the United States by Lake Book Manufacturing, LLC
The text stock is SFI certified. The Sustainable Forestry Initiative® program
promotes sustainable forest management.

10 9 8 7 6 5 4 3 2 1

Text design and layout by Virginia Scott Bowman
This book was typeset in Garamond Premier Pro with Kepler and Trenda used as
display typefaces

To send correspondence to the author of this book, mail a first-class letter to the
author c/o Inner Traditions • Bear & Company, One Park Street, Rochester, VT
05767, and we will forward the communication, or contact the author directly at
paintingtheparanormal.com.

For music lovers everywhere.

Swamiji under study by the government of India Medical Institute in New Dehli. Here he is shown drumming on one breath in an airtight chamber for thirty-five minutes.

Contents

❖ · · · · ❖

Preface

I heard a new sound: a living sound, like the richest, most complex, most beautiful piece of music you've ever heard.

EBEN ALEXANDER, M.D., *PROOF OF HEAVEN*

THIS IS A BOOK ABOUT MUSIC, but a special kind of music we'll call *transcendental.* In what sense I use this term will get clearer as we proceed. Two notable experiences led me to write about the extraordinary Indian musician, Nada Brahmananda, whom I first met in 1976. One was an apparent precognitive dream about Nada before I ever heard of him. The other took place five years before I met the Swami, perhaps the strangest experience I've ever had that centered around a piece of music I'd call transcendental. So I should begin with an account of this experience, written down soon after it happened:

I live on the top floor of 14 Bedford Street in the West Village of New York City with my partner, Jane. We are listening to a jazz composition by John Coltrane, The Father and the Son and the Holy Ghost. *It is about 11:30 p.m. Jane is sprawled out on the sofa. I step to the window and gaze vacantly into the clear evening sky. I'm in a mild reverie from Coltrane's hypnotic beat, softly thumping my foot, swaying to the rhythms of the music.*

Suddenly, a cluster of dazzling white lights appears out of nowhere. The lights are larger and more brilliant than any stars. They are attached to nothing I can see. They perform zigzag aerial acrobatics, in tune, it seems, with Coltrane's music. Their appearance in the sky is so sudden and so silent, I just keep staring, somewhat surprised, listening to the music, watching the dance of lights. After about twenty seconds I realize that what I'm seeing is very strange indeed, and it starts to sink in. Something outside my window a few hundred or so feet in the sky seems to be communing with me and the music of John Coltrane.

My attention fixed on the dancing lying light-cluster, I yell to Jane to come to the window. She gives a start, and joins me. Apparently I'm not just "seeing" things. Jane puts on her glasses and raises the window. It's no reflection. Something is really out there, brighter, more dazzling, than any star. The light-entity suddenly stops its aerial capers and slowly glides downward, in a straight line, toward the dome of Our Lady of Pompei, the oldest church in Greenwich Village—built more than a century ago to serve migrants and refugees, located to the right at the corner of Carmine and Bleecker Streets.

The lights hover there, pulsing above the dome of the church. An unusual sensation comes over me; it feels like I'm flying far out in space, surrounded by stars. Among the stars, I see the dome of Our Lady of Pompei and the lights still pulsing.

Then I realize I am back in my room. The church is just blocks away! But now something else. Over the lights I see—but this more inwardly than outwardly—two large heads and massive shoulders. The figures I see look excited! They're *watching us! I recall one of the heads. It was human. I get an impression of curiosity, a kind of playful agitation, and a strong feeling that I—and Jane, who was half-dressed—are the objects of voyeuristic curiosity.*

Suddenly, the impression of the two heads fades. My attention is *again riveted on the church dome. The light entity, above the cross, still pulsing, suddenly shoots back to where we first saw it, a few hundred feet above our rooftop. Again it makes zany and impossible aerial maneuvers. Then, without warning, it stops and hop-flies across the skyline, going uptown. We observe its trajectory, scramble to the other window, and watch it take one last curving leap over the top of the Empire State Building where it vanishes.**

Jane and I were electrified after this highly strange encounter with what nowadays is called a UAP, an unidentified aerial phenomenon. Our apartment was on the top floor and we both had the impulse to walk a flight up and step onto the roof, which we promptly did. There we met with an equally astonished person, a young drummer who lived in the same apartment building, and whom I had recently turned on to the music of John Coltrane. His name was Louie and he said, "Did you see that?" So we had a third witness to confirm that what we saw was "real." Louie noted the silence of our visitor and saw the lights in the form of a pyramid. Neither Jane nor I had had any impression of a pyramid.

The presence of a third witness was striking, connecting us all under the rubric of music; moreover, otherworldly, ecstatic music that demands intense concentration. Without the right receptivity, listening to that particular composition of Coltrane's might be unbearable. It crossed my mind that the concentrated state of Jane's and my minds listening to Coltrane, along with a sympathetic Louie on the roof, may have somehow resonated with an unknown agency "out there" that caused our experience. I wondered if maybe we had attracted whatever it was to ourselves. But what *was* it? To this day, I do not know, and the mystery remains.

Subsequent inquiry left us as the apparently sole witnesses to the

---

*See chapter 4 in my book *Soulmaking,* Anomalist Books.

visitation. Nothing on the news and no gossip in the neighborhood indicated otherwise. Whatever the light entity was, it seemed to know what we were listening to, and was dancing or somehow interacting with us. When it went to the dome of Our Lady of Pompei, beamed and pulsated, and then came back to where it first appeared, it was letting us know it knew what we were listening to—John Coltrane's wildly avant-garde riff on the Father and the Son and the Holy Ghost. What we saw was something more like a winged thought than a physical craft. No physical craft with anything resembling a human organism could perform the movements in space that we observed. Whatever it was that we saw was intelligent, aware of what we were doing, and unconstrained by physical space and reality. And it chose to connect with us via the language of music, light, and dance.

The timing was rife with synchronicities. It was Jane's birthday, April 23. How many of us can boast of receiving such a birthday present? This date is also William Shakespeare's birthday. For me the timing was also pregnant with meaning; I was five days away from defending my doctoral thesis in philosophy at Columbia University. I was about to become a "doctor" of philosophy, as it were, officially certified wise and learned. Was there some cosmic joker cruising around on the lookout for human subjects that need humbling? Was the message, *Figure us out, doctor of philosophy!?*

I wondered about the music. During Socrates's last conversations with friends just before his execution, he admitted to having a recurrent dream, which he was still having even in prison.[1] The dream kept telling him he had to "make music." So a certain Socratic doubt about the kind of philosophy I wanted to practice crept into my consciousness. Speaking of dreams, I should now describe my precognitive dream of a funny man who offered to teach me music. There would be no instruments, he told me. *No instruments? Meaning what?* So there was something about music that was prodding me. Between Coltrane being somehow linked to my close encounter with a UAP, Socrates's mysterious dream on the threshold of his death, and my own dream about music, thoughts of music kept nagging me.

Around that time, I was working uptown on 71st Street at the then all-women Catholic Marymount Manhattan College. I taught philosophy, a possibly subversive enterprise, so the nuns kept their eyes on me as I kept my eyes on the student body. The seventies were turbulent times in New York City, and things came to a head in 1977 with the historic blackout of most of the five boroughs on July 13.

A bolt of lightning hit a power station, sparking a chain reaction that cut the power off and threw the city into darkness and chaos. Trains in subways and elevators in buildings came to a halt, while in some poor neighborhoods looting and fires broke out. Wild gunfights in near darkness between police and populace occurred, but somehow not one person was even wounded.

It was a collective psychic explosion, amplified by foul weather. Since 1975, New York City, had been nearly bankrupt, and Mayor Abe Beame begged the federal government for financial assistance. President Ford famously replied, "No way!" The city was down in the dumps, so to speak; cops, firefighters, and teachers were striking and morale was low. Crime, dirt, despair, graffiti, and the blackout spoke loudly of unemployment, corruption, and the discontent of a suffering city.

The looters were pragmatic and stole the audio equipment they needed to become DJs—they wanted, they needed to project their voices and their music into the ambient public spaces. After the blackout, DJs popped up all over the city and spread beyond, jump-starting disco and punk, hip hop and rap, all bursting on the scene around 1977. It was a time when new styles, narratives, and rhythms of music were flourishing despite—or maybe because of—all the unrest and discontent.

The music and the equipment and the DJs gave birth to dance clubs that became scenes of near-Dionysian abandon—enclaves of high decibel, stroboscopic, whirling bodies, magnified by drugs and catering to the polymorphous perverse. In the eyes of Billy Graham and his flock, it was Sodom and Gomorrah, but to the young and the disaffected, it meant ecstasy and liberation. New York was in a state of upheaval, a low point in its history; it was a city ravaged by greed, crime, and poverty.

But into all this landed a roly-poly monk-musician, a homeless mystic and immigrant from Mysore, India. A visitor, smiling, some might say, from another planet. The word *ghandarva* means "celestial musician," a term used to describe this monk, well-known in India, a world-traveler who would eventually return to Rishikesh, his home ashram in the Himalayas.

In the 1970s he was living in New York City at 243 West 24th Street, the Shivananda Yoga Vedanta Center. What follows is a record of my experiences with this remarkable man. That I should meet him seemed curious, given the powerful feelings I was having about music, and about Socrates's dream that told him to make music.

Soon after my dream of the strange musician, my friend Alida told me of a certain esoteric sound yoga she was studying with, a person called Swami Nada Brahmananda. She sparked my curiosity, so I made an appointment for a lesson. This was in the spring of 1976, and from then to the summer of 1979, I got to know and spend time with Swami Nada. I recorded the lessons I took with him and promptly typed them up, thinking it would be wise to keep a written record. I had discovered a very unusual man who possessed some very unusual ideas and abilities.

Interested in Nada's art form of sacred rhythms and vibrations, I managed, barely, to learn to chant, drum, and play the harmonium. I had at the same time begun playing the flute. Besides the mysteries of sacred music, I was interested in getting to know the monk as a person—his story, his beliefs, what he was feeling and thinking. He was a master of a rare type of music yoga—called *taan,* or vibration yoga—grounded in a tradition that dates back thousands of years. I soon learned that he cheerfully believed we are deep into the *Kali Yuga,* at the end of a human cycle, a time when *Moksha* or spiritual enlightenment was unusually difficult to achieve. During the decadent Age of Kali, the yoga of music was thought to be the best way to pursue enlightenment.

Music can take hold of our consciousness in special ways, and be used to break the dark spell that is the Kali Yuga. At its best, music can elevate our consciousness, and do it in a way that moralizing and dogmatizing cannot. Cultural traditions often rely on music to induce higher, often therapeutic, states of mind. Much of the great music of the West, from Palestrina to Bach, to John Coltrane, can lift our spirits out of the lowlands of consciousness. But now, here comes Nada Brahmananda.

1

Laughing Master
from a Dream

WALKING UPTOWN THIS AFTERNOON from my apartment in the
West Village toward the Sivananda Ashram, I was feeling jaunty in
spite of the piles of garbage that had yet to be collected, lined up on the
curb for blocks and blocks in both directions.

My friend Alida told me about Swami Nada Brahmananda, and I
was curious to meet him whose advent was heralded to me in a dream.
Upon arrival at the ashram on 24th Street, I noticed four words inscribed
on the door of the old brownstone: "Serve, Love, Meditate, Realize."

Stepping inside, I saw a spot where shoes were neatly placed
together. I removed my shoes, and followed a sign pointing upstairs
that said "This Way for Music Students." I noticed on the bulletin
board a photograph of Swami Vishnu, a smallish muscular guy, doing
a headstand on the edge of a rooftop somewhere in New York City.
He'd make a great Hollywood stunt man, I thought.

"Michael?" Swami Nada called out when I knocked on the door
upstairs. My lesson was for five o'clock, and I was on time. I didn't
expect to hear my name called out that way, as if the man inside had
known me for years.

"I wasn't sure if I should knock," I said, entering.

"No, no," he said, his voice warmly resonant, "this is your time."

A young woman with a guitar, about to leave, made a gesture of obeisance, which seemed awkward. I imagined myself performing a similar gesture, but the idea made me uncomfortable. I decided to approach the venerable Swami in as natural and direct a way as I would anybody else.

"Come Michael," he said, and pointed to an empty place beside him on the floor. There were no chairs in the room. The lessons were conducted on the floor, student and teacher sitting beside one another. I could see he was not tall, and fat would be the wrong word—compactly roundish might be better. He was an eighty-one-year-old with the fresh glossy skin of a child and a welcoming face. His eyes were especially penetrating.

The small room was brightly lit and fragrant with incense. The walls displayed several posters of popular Indian religious art. On the mantel of a stopped fireplace stood a photograph of Swami Nada with Swami Muktananda, a holy man I once met in upstate New York for an interview that was unsatisfactory. Muktananda sat on a platform above me and preached but hardly replied to any of my questions.

I sat down beside Swami Nada, as I would come to call him. He let me know I could study whatever I wished to learn from him, be it vocal, tabla, or harmonium. He had taught people around the world: famous musicians, monks, beggars, pundits, politicians, hysterics, and children barely out of their diapers. He described a boy of eight years whom he was teaching in New York City, a superior musician to his mother.

He suggested that this lady was afflicted with "brain trouble." I took him to mean she was some kind of neurotic. The boy's facility had nothing to do with anything akin to personal talent but was the result of karmic residues from previous lifetimes. Unknown to Nada's vocabulary was the flattering epithet *talented*.

I remarked that I was happy, and felt lucky to have met him. Again he explained, it wasn't chance but actions from a previous life that led me to his feet. And he added, quite casually, I and generations of my offspring were now in a position to receive *moksha*—release from all our bad karma. This notion that were I to achieve liberation in this life my offspring would be so privileged, seemed a wee bit unreasonable; it was like original sin only in reverse. But then, I suppose, I ought not to have taken him so literally.

He seemed glad to impart to me a feeling of great optimism, also perhaps not to be taken quite so literally. So I nodded and smiled. The last thing I wanted was to inhibit the flow, the music of his thoughts with rationalistic quibbles. Part of the lesson, I realized, was to allow myself to absorb his meaning by being fully present to the man, even to ideas he had that might seem to me fantastic and incredible.

"Can I tell you," I said, "I dreamt a dream some days before I heard of you. I dreamt I was on a ship and getting a music lesson from a man of some years who was very funny. He told me there would be no instruments. Was it you that I met in my dream?"

I wasn't sure if he understood me; Nada's store of English was scanty.

"You see," I went on, once I saw he understood, "I already have a music teacher—a flute teacher. Then Alida called and told me about you! A different kind of teacher, she said. So what I'm saying. . . ." I paused and noticed I had his full attention. "It's as if you called me from the future! Impossible, but it happened!"

I tried to convey to him what I felt about precognition, the enigma of time and the riddle of backward causation. And I was curious to see if he would be pleased when I recounted my apparently precognitive dream. He nodded but said nothing.

Parvati, Nada's young disciple from California, entered the room, smiled, bent down, and picked up a cup. I noticed the way she moved as she stooped without bending her knees, stretching her limbs, as if she were letting some invisible spirit flow through her. She seemed earnest about not wasting a single gesture, not missing a single opportunity to perform an act of devotion to her Divine Self—embodied in her master, Swami Nada. After lighting a fresh stick of incense, she stole silently from the room, and I was alone again with the master of sound yoga.

Alida had mentioned he was on in years, but the bald-shaven, portly monk that sat before me had a baby face. His brown eyes possessed a liquid sparkle that suggested the labile temperament of a child; at the same time, they could suddenly appear quite fiercely focused. The lines in the palm of his left hand were shaped distinctly like the Star of David, as if the design were impressed there deliberately. I asked if I could have a closer look at the palm of his hand. Obligingly, he rested his hand in mine and allowed me to inspect it. The hand that lay in mine seemed uncannily weightless, and the perfect star could have been etched by Albrecht Durer.

I was wondering how the lesson would begin when he suddenly remarked, sounding carefully chosen words, rhythmically and emphatically: "Mind control is life, rhythm is music."

These seven words I was ready to embrace as my mantra. Nada spoke little English—in a way, an advantage. He was forced to distill his thoughts into compressed formulas. It would be part of my lessons to unpack his meanings, catch the feel of the way he said things, the pulse and tempo of his insights.

Mind control is life. Much wisdom was couched in those simple words—it was practically a summary of classical Greek philosophy. One unguarded moment, one wrong rush of feeling, one too-hasty deed that spirals out of control, and we are in somebody's tragedy or comedy.

Nada's method for getting mind control and rhythm was *to count*. So he showed me how to count *tala keherawa,* a rhythmic pattern of four beats. He clapped on the first beat and then brought three successive fingers beginning with the pinky down on the final three beats of the *tala.*

"One, two, three, four," he began very slowly to intone. A wave of calm swept over me. He counted again, and as he counted he peered at me. I became transfixed, as if I were a child. Clapping at a constant beat, each round, he doubled the tempo. After reaching a certain point, he paused and began again, this time using the Sanskrit syllables, *dhagi, natin, naka, dhina.* He kept doubling the tempo until the audible syllables faded into a slur of infinity. He did this without any sign of effort.

He stopped again and showed me an album with photographs of himself on his travels, pointing to many notable people, kings and holy men and astronauts and famed musicians. He lingered over each photograph and seemed to enjoy reliving the moments the camera had captured.

Again we went back to counting. This time he suggested that I count with him. I clapped at the wrong beat. Instantly he stopped and said, chuckling, "What you think then?"

"Wondering about my first mistake."

Nada paused and then spoke some more about the benefits of the yoga of music. When my mind wandered, I would make a mistake, and he would instantly catch me. He mimicked a silent meditator, with eyes closed. He decided to critique meditation.

"What meditate?" he said, "thinking Watergate, Nixon, business? Oh yes, very good but sleeping—and nobody catch!"

He had a point. On the other hand, once the counting became automatic, you could go back to thinking about Nixon and other monumental ephemera.

Again we proceeded to count together, and as we approached the fourth doubling of the tempo, my tongue got twisted and I lost the thread. We went back to the beginning, this time very slowly.

"Full mind need," Nada said.

His remark that *mind control was life* was reverberating in my head. I began to feel uncomfortable at the prospect of making mistakes, and at the same time was resisting the idea of having to concentrate so hard.

I might fail, my inner imp whispered. And with that thought I lost control and screwed up again. A surprising effect of Nada's teaching—I was dwelling on the idea that my life or death hung on a thought!

"Alida say you Ph.D.," he said.

"Yes," I said, wishing to avoid the subject.

He eyed me with curiosity.

"What you get, what grade? Eighty percent? Ninety percent?"

I shrugged.

"Ninety-nine-point-nine percent you *fail* with me!" he said cheerfully.

He started to count again. Relentlessly, he corrected me. He intended that I get it right. I soon learned that once he started to teach me something, he would not let me go unless I got it. Despite his jovial nature, Nada taught as if it were indeed a matter of life and death that I get my mind and my rhythm right. This made me uneasy, and my hands began to sweat. I felt like going home and practicing by myself. I told him this in so many words and he laughed and looked at me sternly.

"How you learn without master?" he asked.

Each time I got one thing right he found something else wrong—not bringing my hand up to my ear, not intoning correctly. Learning to count to four with Nada was no easy matter. I slipped and used my index finger—he took my hand and shook it forbiddingly.

"Never this finger, this ego finger, always pointing, want this, do that," he said.

I was about to explain to the Swami the meaning of the middle finger in New Jersey, but checked myself.

I really began to doubt if I would make it into the divine groove that day. My mind was racing, and Nada was watching me like a hawk with his dagger-sharp eyes. He seemed to sense my mounting frustration and said, "Michael, I love you—but in this, *no love.*" This remark pulled me back and I finally got it right.

"Correct," he said jubilantly.

I gave a sigh of relief. For a moment I felt composed. Nada leaned over, pulled the harmonium toward him, and began to play and chant, his eyes half-closed, his face transformed. He seemed to withdraw into another world. He sang with every iota of his soul. He might have been alone or before an audience of thousands. He was afloat in the beyond on sounding wings of ecstasy. His voice was soft, almost inaudible now, and I sensed a current of vibrant energy emanating from him.

I had read that the Swami could sing from different parts of his body, from the root of his spine and the apex of his skull, and had seen photographs of scientists poking about with microphones at the extremities of his body, confirming his claims. The man was a human vibrator, I thought. Nada's instrument was his body; he played it and made it sing.

I flashed on my dream. *No instruments,* the funny old teacher had said. Nada's instrument was himself—every thought, every cell, every muscle. He sat there as if he were trilling divine arpeggios from his fingertips. I closed my eyes and felt waves of sound transform into feeling, remembering the line from Wallace Stevens, that "Music is feeling, then, not sound."[1] I followed Nada's "feeling" through a dark, widening corridor that opened to a luminous landscape. The voice of the singing swami liquefied my nerves, melting, it seemed, the hardness of bone and muscle. It was as if the center of myself had slipped from the envelope of my body and fanned out and was floating in the space around me. Was this what moksha was all about? You get melted down and spaced out? You sail on the crest of a wave that never breaks?

Suddenly he doubled the tempo, bringing me back, and then again, and once more, and his voice trailed off into spirals of infinity. Nada was demonstrating how far one could go by learning how to count to four. He suddenly stopped, turned toward me, and smiled. Clearly, it pleased him to indulge his virtuosic caper.

"I happy, God happy—you happy," he said.

I nodded with amazement at his gorgeous idea of divine conviviality.

"*Raga yaman,*" he observed, commenting on the song he had just sung. "Lakshmi give us money and food."

The song was an incantation to a helping mother goddess. This could seem like just magic, but Nada at once shifted his meaning.

"Request," he said, "and mother Lakshmi give us money and food. Very easy! When much money, then ego coming. When more money coming—what then? Who are you? I don't know. Very good friend—no more, no more."

The way he said "who are you?" I felt the rhythm of his mind; he was neither moralizing nor preaching. Nada lived his philosophy through his songs. I also got the impression that the smiling monk had known a few fair-weather friends. But any real bitterness by now seemed under control in the crucible of his musical *sadhana.*

He sang and heart-felt pangs mildly convulsed the muscles of his face, noticeably around his eyes and his mouth. His voice seemed softly to gather and rise from a great internal depth. Now he stopped singing, his hand on the harmonium, holding a plaintive chord.

"*Ramanar bissara bunde, khali ana khali jana.* Empty coming, empty going, only God's name is sure, before and now and after." The vibrations made by the song were their lived presence, and for Nada, their vibrant truth.

Nada went on to outline his picture of human life. The master metaphor was "school." Every stranger met on the way was a teacher; every situation you encounter a test of your spirit and a lesson to be learned. The universe is a hierarchy of classes, semesters, graduations, or getting "left back," as they said when I was a kid in grade school. Nada was the perfect schoolmaster for the ultimate education of the soul. "This life, use correct—then you getting moksha, no birth, no death."

According to the Indian guru, life is a journey in the school of self-transformation. My feelings toward the metaphor were mixed: I liked it because it hinted at great vistas of experiment and experience; at the same time, I had misgivings. I've never been a very good student. I manage but always blunder along in my own eccentric way.

"Not use correct," my new teacher announced. "What you getting? Punishment, eighty-four million lives going again. Pass examination, you get degree. Fail, very bad! Very bad!"

"*Really?*" I said, starting to squirm a little. Did I really have to go back to school? Could it really take eighty-four million lives before I graduate? I thought I had escaped school once and for all. At my desk in grade school, I excelled in gazing at clouds adrift in the sky. I felt a secret kinship with their aimless movements. I tried to explain to Nada that I was a rebellious student, and never showed up at any of my graduation ceremonies, high school or college. Music to me was the sound of the bell shouting that class was over.

Nada smiled and put his hand on my shoulder.

"Practice music, Michael," he said earnestly, "this is not entertainment, not for others—this is for your Self."

When he actually said, "Practice music, Michael," I instantly remembered what Socrates was told in his recurrent dream: "Make music, and practice hard!"

Nada described all the advantages that would accrue if I followed the path he said was true and best. To begin with, health and happiness would be mine. The main thing was to obey the rules in the art of living and to secure a right understanding of the fundamental principles. The rest was just practice—again, I recalled Socrates, who said that philosophy was a form of "practice" (*melete,* in Greek). In the end, I'd be able to smile in the face of life and death, like a real master, comfortably one with my higher Self.

Nada explained that unenlightened death was like going through a revolving door that let you back in the same big department store with countless rooms and myriads of distracting commodities to suck you in. He made a comical gesture of trying to get out through the door but always being pushed back in. He gaped at me with mock astonishment. Through all this, the drone of the harmonium was continuous, as if to underline the constancy of the all-witnessing Self through the endless comings and goings, appearings and disappearings, of our time-tossed existence.

He sang a little more, then broke in on himself, fingers still dancing over the keys of the harmonium. Musing on the words of the song, he said: "Flowers, very beautiful; face, very beautiful—what you getting? Cemetery!" and resumed singing *a tempo*. Gee, I thought, that wasn't exactly an upbeat intermezzo.

An elderly lady who spoke with a French accent entered without knocking.

"Come in, mother," said Nada, whose custom, I would learn, was to address all women as "mother."

My time was finished. I got up and the French lady sat down beside Nada, praising him effusively, pawing him as if he were a teddy bear.

"Isn't he marvelous?" she said, peering up at me with unabashed awe.

"You *are* marvelous," she said again, turning to Nada, clutching him wantonly, "you just *know* you are."

I detected pique in his eyes, but he allowed the good-natured matron to envelop him with her affection.

"You *do* keep yourself well—come here," she said to me, "look at his teeth—what *amazing* teeth!"

The affable monk opened his mouth, smiled primly, and displayed his teeth.

Dazed, and feeling a bit giddy, I stumbled out the door, thanking Swami Nada for the rigorous, enlightening lesson. Half-way down the stairs it occurred to me I forgot to leave the ten dollars for my lesson. Alida mentioned that four of the ten went to Nada and Parvati—not much—and the other six to the True World Order, or, as devotees called it, the Organization. I went back and placed a ten dollar bill on top of the bureau. Nada's face brightened when I stepped in, apparently unaware of the reason, and said, as I left the second time: "From now on you going up! . . . up! . . . up!"

2

Learning by Heart

I WAS EARLY FOR THE LESSON TODAY and so sat down on the floor in the library of the ashram. Voices and soft drumbeats floated down from the rooms upstairs.

"*Tala* means balance," Nada had said during the first lesson. *Was I balanced?* I asked myself. I remembered a dream of mine: I'm climbing a mountain, I reach a narrow pass, a ledge begins to slip, the ground beneath gives way. That dream seems to have said something about me not being very balanced at all.

Waiting for my music lesson, I pictured Socrates in the days before his trial and execution, awkwardly trying to dance to a lyric he invented about one of Aesop's fables. Socrates was concerned not to slight any of the gods on the eve of his departure to the *allos topos* ("other place"). Best to pay all debts to gods and powers before heading out into unknown afterlife terrain. So the canny talker is up on his haunches dancing, singing, and trying to make music. After all, a dream had told him to. . . .

"You can go up now," Parvati said, as she passed by the door of the library.

Swami Nada welcomed me. Today we sang together for the first time. Without warning he began, fusing a single relaxed breath to a syllable, in a succession of three—*sa pa sa*—ascending and descending in octaves. This was followed by a repetition of the same notes, but instead of *sa pa sa*, he only sang *ah ah ah*. He did this several times, very slowly and deliberately. Making the gesture, he became totally immersed in it. It seemed to me that it made no difference to Nada whether he was singing three simple notes or a complex song with rapidly changing rhythms and meanings. His act was complete in either case; what he did seemed always to proceed from the center of his being, always in unison with his whole self.

Nada could afford to be capricious, I thought, as long as he was anchored in his deep self. At first I was baffled by his slowness and deliberateness. He asked me to chant *sa pa sa* with him. He seemed to be coming from elsewhere, floating in another space, and I was confused. But soon enough, I relaxed into the flow and heard the pattern. He praised me and said one of his favorite expressions: I came correct.

Coming correct means being right on, on time, well-timed, ordered in time, but also timeless. The root of being in tune with time is the mind, mind in touch with itself, in rhythmic concord with itself as it flows onward. As I would gradually learn, for Nada, any incident of life might be an occasion for "coming correct." Indeed, infinite are the ways one can come correct—or not. The sweetness and bitterness were everywhere to be tasted.

After doing *sa pa sa* for a while we stopped and he exclaimed, almost as an afterthought: "Do it. It opens all the chakras."

The remark surprised me. I had always thought of the opening process being gradual, step by step, like going up a ladder. Something like Plato's ladder of love that you ascend—orderly and linear. But Nada's mind thought of opening all the chakras in one fell swoop, chakras being those focal points of bodily life that are gateways to higher forms of consciousness. Coming correct is a big deal. Nada doesn't use big words like "enlightenment." Instead, he played the chord and held it, our identities blended in the oneness of the chord.

We then went on to sing a scale, first he alone and then I with him. *Sa ri ga ma pa da ni sa,* and then back, *sa ni da pa ma ga ri sa.* I proceeded cautiously but stumbled. The trick was to feel the whole scale, not as a series of separate components but as continuous, as if it had a life of its own.

Swami Nada asked me to imitate a raga he sang on the harmonium. I managed about half of it and then lost the thread. I wished for a sheet of music, notes written out in space, in clear linear order. I needed a map. I complained about missing paper and written symbols!

"What is paper?" he said sternly. "Paper is paper. It is something outside of you. Not you. Always paper, paper. With all this paper you will never be master, never free. It must be inside you. Then you are master. Learn by heart. Then good is easy, automatic. Flute will follow fingers, fingers follow heart. Listen and learn by heart."

Listen and learn by heart. Five simple words. They struck home with great power. Was there a message here about a philosopher's endeavor to recover his heart, to understand the secret of learning by heart—and with heart?

"People do not know, this is Kali Yuga," Nada said with a tone of great earnestness.

"What is that?" I asked.

"Now," he said, "people use paper, instead of Self. Very bad time. What is down coming up. What is up coming down. Men forget God and always fighting. Don't know why. Just fighting—animals never fighting like that."

Kali Yuga is the age of absconded gods. A time of learning without heart, information without insight; a time of paper and print, money and marriage license, diploma and death certificate. Kali Yuga, as Nada saw it, implied servitude to gadgets, machines, clocks, calendars, all the artificial distinctions that mar the musical flow of the divine way of being.

"In the beginning," he went on, "in Krtayuga, no paper, no reading, no writing—just Truth."

Wait a second! Reliance upon nothing? Just Truth? I was devastated by this simplicity. Truth—oh, that! Just the bare brilliant consciousness of the true being of all there is! What could be simpler? I was curious to ask about Truth, but he continued.

"Then there was a little reading and writing, and there was less Truth," he added. Progressively, we degenerate. Paper and more paper and the collective memory of the true Self is estranged, weakens, and finally fades to nothing. A once living tradition decays and, in effect, becomes extinct. And so, as Ammon, the Egyptian king, long ago prophesied, the invention of letters would force men to rely on outer things, and would create elaborate and complicated illusions of knowledge.

In early times, Nada believed, human beings were in touch with the great saving Truth. It is no easy task to rescue the lost jewel of the Self from beneath the debris of modern print culture—but Nada held to a strand of optimism.

"In Kali Yuga, music is the way," he said.

I asked why this was so, and he replied that almost every human being loves some kind of music. Music casts a spell on the mind by virtue of tala or rhythm, which is the soul of all kinds of music. Tala also means balance, which implies the need for rhythmic control. I should add that tala or balance was a highly generalized concept for Swami Nada, which he applied to all aspects of the art of living. Under the spell of music—however fleeting—we can begin, if only for the length of a song, to transcend our divided selves.

Nada's music was meant to lift the veil of ordinary consciousness. Things of a higher order wait to be seen and heard. Victims of the belief-tyrannies of Kali Yuga, entangled by the coils of Maya, want to wrench themselves free. Nada's view was that music has the power to wrench us free. Other methods, he argued, are less compelling. For example, when you do ordinary pranayama, or breathing exercises, you might get bored and just go to sleep. But with nada yoga, exercising the breath means making sounds that tell stories that resonate with the deep chords of the soul. Music stirs our energy and personality more than rational discourse, which is a more abstract process. Our will may waver, our mind may get cloudy; but the energy of music can clarify the mind and inspire the will. Music puts us in touch with the more vital zones of our being. "Music is the way," Nada repeated, "in Kali Yuga."

I was thinking of the powerful connection between breath and altered states of consciousness. Breath, in Greek, is *psyche,* the mysterious word that means soul. What is soul? According to Heraclitus, it is somewhere whose boundaries you will never discover, no matter which way or how far you travel. By controlling your breath you can control your consciousness. That is a fact that some people turn into miracles.

Nada showed me a new rhythmic pattern, *tala dadara,* six beats. *Datin dadha tona,* one, two, three, four, five, six. My hand was to pause on the clap till the count of three and four was complete. Involuntarily, it shot up too soon. Gently he held my hand, a patient father, and laughed lightly: "You come too quickly," he said in perfect English.

You old rascal, I smiled to myself. That's why everybody likes music. The pleasure of music was also the gift of Eros.

"You never used written sheets of music?" I asked, still reluctant to believe it was so.

"I never read a book," he said, "I, zero in school."

Wow, I thought. "Not even a music book?"

"No paper," he remarked, "you write what I know by heart—yes, fill two trucks, fill two trucks with paper. But paper teach you nothing. I teach you." Nada's psyche was his internet. It felt like my time was up. It was a good lesson. I got a further glimpse of a rare type of human being, a person whose cultural identity was fashioned from materials of preliterate and prescientific times. It was like taking lessons from a three-thousand-year-old man. And I walked away with a more vivid sense of what it means to "learn by heart."

3

The Inner Saboteur

I ARRIVED AT THE ASHRAM EARLY, confident, thinking I'd be singing. I was convinced that I had "mastered" tala keherawa, the most elementary rhythm in Indian music. I had been practicing tala dadara, and was able to count out the rhythm; but coordinating the motions of my hands with the counting was difficult. Mind and body were reluctant to cooperate and synchronize. I could count and I could move my hands. But to perform both actions in harmony was something else. A child could do it, I thought, but the exercise became a screen where I watched myself project doubt and hesitation. That would complicate the lesson.

"Count, tala keherawa," the master said. So, I thought, back to that elementary stuff. I began to count. Nada tapped his fingers on the sides of the harmonium along with me. And what did it matter, anyway, if I made an ordinary mistake? There was something else I had to confront. I hope I'm not alone in this regard, but I discovered early on a curious phenomenon, something inside me that *wanted* me to make mistakes. It seemed to enjoy throwing obstacles my way. An alien entity, an uninvited guest—but seemingly quite real. I call it my "inner saboteur." I don't know if this is just a figure of speech or another name for the more active side of what C. G. Jung called the Shadow. I've always viewed Jung's Shadow as lurking in the dark background and discreetly wreaking havoc on innocent bystanders. My Inner Saboteur is an active and blatantly perverse agency. Give it a chance, an opening, and it will spring on me with shameless gusto.

Mistakes began to pile up. But Nada's voice and the rhythmic tapping had the effect of altering my consciousness, dilating my sense of time, and increasing the flow of my imagery.

"Again," he said, "must come correct, get balance—you come little late, little soon."

I felt trapped. He was not going to let me out of the ashram until I got it correct. I could end up stranded here forever!

I really wanted to leave. In the back of my mind I preferred to rely on myself because I would then be free to give up, if I felt like it, and do whatever I pleased. There were so many ways to miss the target; the bull's-eye was one lonely spot. A half-hour passed; Nada was relentless. Faster and faster he forced me to return to the beginning, wordless but for an occasional "again." I kept thinking of the eighty-four million reincarnations of misery that lay before me. Temptation to run off waxed, but then waned.

"Must come correct, tala keherawa—that is Life," he pronounced. Most students would take the last remark as a metaphor. I took it literally. If I failed to come correct, I would die! I was standing before Yama, the Great Judge we meet at death, who reads the scroll of our karma. Amid these thoughts I almost made it to the end of the tala but at the last instant the saboteur whispered some low words and I messed up once more.

"I love you, Michael—but in this you must come correct. Now again," Nada said, smiling and then closing his eyes.

"I guess I'm not the best student you ever had." I was pleading before Yama.

He said: "You can make hundreds of mistakes, I not like others."

He imitated the face of an angry, impatient man.

"I not Earth man, never get angry."

He asked if my legs felt stiff, and invited me to stretch. Indeed! Not an Earth man!

Nada rolled up his sari and showed me a scar on his leg.

"Sixty years ago my master put me in hospital. I am not like that."

He wanted to assure me that he had no intention of beating me up. Whew! That was a relief.

Then I got the tala right when we did it together.

"You come correct when I help you. Now do it alone."

"All right, all right," I said.

Finally, I got the whole thing right. The lesson ended, and I complained that I hadn't taken enough time to practice.

"You can practice," he said, "anywhere, walking on Broadway, riding on subway—in latrine. In latrine you practice," he laughed, obviously enjoying his advice. "Nobody bother you in latrine."

Except maybe your Inner Saboteur.

4

Orphic Economics

I WANDERED ABOUT IN GREENWICH VILLAGE the afternoon before my next lesson. I felt a vague longing for something. I felt like trying every restaurant (not that I was hungry), lingering in every bar or coffee shop, like finding the perfect vantage point to watch the everlasting parade of men and women, the colors, the fabulous passings. The mindstuff spun and capered and dispersed over the arabesque of the afternoon. I was everywhere and nowhere.

I hadn't really practiced tala dadara. Nada would catch me again. I ran through some reasons why I might quit taking lessons, but soon found myself edging up Sixth Avenue toward 24th Street.

The ashram seemed strangely desolate; no one in sight, all the doors closed, and there were no sounds. Barefoot I climbed the stairway and began to hear the singing voices of Parvati and Nada. I sat in the dark outside the room where they were doing their practice at the heavenly art. It seemed an endless raga, the melodic lilt rising and falling, drum and harmonium, wave upon wave. Gently, I knocked, since it was my time, but the chanters within were mentally too far away to hear.

I opened the door and sat down. Parvati looked up, slightly startled, and smiled. Nada was spaced out, beyond noticing me. The moment I entered the room, which was brilliantly lit and brimful of incense, I found myself wrapped in a delicate aura of vibrations. I was instantly transported beyond myself, all my moods and gloomy thoughts blown away.

When the song ended Nada began to tell me a story. After a while I gathered it was the story told in the song they were singing. I couldn't quite get the details, but the gist of it came through clear enough. It was about a poor man who was forever chanting. It seems that all around him was poverty and mishap, domestic squabbling, the general woes of everyday existence. But this god-intoxicated raga singer was carefree and high-spirited in the midst of it all.

Swami Nada then pointed out that the poor man comes correct when he chanted because he had nothing to cling to that distracted his mind. He was empty, his mind was light and therefore easy for him to control. "The rich never come correct. Always thinking of business, profit. They sit, fold hands, very silent—but always thinking, always busy."

Nada slapped me on the thigh and chuckled mirthfully.

By this time I had forgotten my anxiety over being tested. Yama had changed into an amiable raconteur of raga-wisdom. Apparently this poor man whose sole occupation was to sing the name of God fell in love with a beautiful maiden who happened to be the king's daughter. Nada paused in his narrative and reminded me that this was a true story.

It occurred to me that moment that he knew or sensed my doubts, my temptation to go wandering through the streets of Greenwich Village. The bedeviled lover was informed that he could marry the king's daughter if he provided her with a dowry of a hundred elephants and a thousand horses. But how could the poor man manage this, since the king alone possessed such fabulous wealth? Well, according to my music teacher, Krishna sent a "cable" that the horses and elephants were on the way. And so the poor chanter got the beauty because he had sung to the gods all his free time, and as an addenda, we learn that the king, with all his treasure, was a clumsy musician who never came correct!

"Poor is good," said Nada, and went on to recount that once he refused money for a performance—would not perform at all—at some place in California because of the presence of some naked ladies. "Were they completely naked?" I asked. "This is not my audience," he said, adding that he was quick to flee from the nest of voluptuaries. I almost blurted out that while I had no craving for riches, I deeply admired some naked ladies, and was sometimes driven to distraction by the need for their company.

Instead I remarked: "I agree about the rich not coming correct— but what if the poor are too poor? What if they are so hungry, they are too weak and too downcast to sing the name of God?"

He instructed me to get up and go to the wall and look at a picture. I went to the wall and there found a photograph of the Sivananda Ashram, set like a jewel in the Himalayas.

"There always chanting, never stop, day and night, always chanting . . . *rama ram hari hari* . . . no money, just song. And they are eating, always food to eat, never hungry. Lions and tigers are in and out going. Nothing special. Food is coming in, and nobody working— only singing night and day."

This is too good to be true, I thought to myself. I tried to imagine it occurring somewhere in the Bronx where I spent my days as a poor student of City College.

He made the further point that nobody owns the wealth of the world, the food, the air, the animals; that all comes from God and who-ever sings the name of God will be fed by God. Food finds its way to the ashram and all who wish to lodge there and chant can do so. Even the wild animals of mountain and jungle come and go in peace. The idea of this orphic economics was outrageously impractical just about anywhere on Earth. At the same time it stirred the utopian fantast in me, sparking images of cosmic harmony, mystic joy, and plenitude.

"But Swamiji," I protested, "it won't work here. Our world is different. When you go to the supermarket you must pay hard cash—

if not, what you get is jail! They'll put Swami in a cage, and throw away the key."

"No," he said, refusing to yield the point, "here stop—change, people listening, change!"

"I suppose it's possible, if you're incredibly good—but no one is likely to feed *me* for singing the name of God in public. More likely, I'd be arrested for disturbing the peace."

"Then practice more," he said, smiling, knowing he had me on that point.

I was forming a picture of what it was to be a ghandarva, or celestial musician—a wanderer who owns nothing and sings the names of divine power. I thought about the time—it looked like there would be no music lesson, at least in the usual sense. Just when I was thinking of time, Nada reached for an alarm clock that was sitting beside him and held it up before me.

"This is mud," he said flatly. I didn't quite understand what he meant, but the image struck me as funny and I laughed. Time, he must have meant, was mud. Nada laughed too, even though I wasn't sure what either of us were laughing about. Then he pointed to the table and said: "Mud."

I was slow in seeing what he was driving at. Strange music lesson!

"Food is mud," he added, "flesh is mud, all go back to mud." Okay. Got it. Everything is mortal, transient, time-driven, and therefore, in the end, returns to the mud and dust of material ruin. So why worry? We're not part of that, being portions of the mind of God. Whether we know it or not, we are, at bottom, free spirits.

"Earth, you mean—everything comes from and returns to the Earth."

"Earth," he said, but apparently preferred mud.

"In this mud-world, everything is mud," he continued with a jolly air. Again, his blanket dismissal of everything as mud was very funny, and we laughed once more. Nada enjoyed me enjoying his remarks, and we got into a kind of contest of mirth. Aroused, he launched into a catalogue of pronouncements concerning the mud essence of all phenomena. And he made the rant rhythmical—kings and queens are mud, nightclubs and whiskey, politicians and professors, and so on and so forth. We all die as we came into the world, empty-handed. Ergo, it's all mud and the song of God.

By this time it was six o'clock and the next student was knocking on the door. I was about to get up and leave when he said: "I test you now—sing *sa pa sa*."

I intoned the three notes up and down several times. Silent, he listened attentively.

"Correct!" he said, delighted that I had done it right. "You pass! Not come back eighty-four million times!"

The man who was not from Earth was applying a gentle spur of encouragement. I was grateful, and started to leave. He called after me and remarked that I had better believe everything he said. Doubt, he reminded me, was death. He advised me to stay away from nightclubs, sexy women, whiskey, gambling, and so forth. Stay home and practice— sadhana was where it was at. He was moved to lay one further bit of practical advice on me: "When walking—stop for red light—not stop, go to hospital!" He smiled warmly and added, just as I slipped out of the door: "But remember—the world is mud."

5

The High Cost of Perfection

NADA MADE FUN OF PEOPLE who moved around a lot during his performances. He objected to swaying in unison with the music. To me it was the natural thing to do; for him it was a sign of disrespect and lack of understanding. To illustrate his point, he told me a story.

Once upon a time there was a great king, Akbar. It was the singing-time of Tansen, master magician of mantras, and there was a big program in the king's palace. On one side the officers and ministers sat, on the other, the king's friends and family. Each person was dressed according to their rank and station. It was not like a program at the ashram in New York, Nada said, where people wore whatever they felt like wearing, saffron robes or threadbare blue jeans.

Nobody would dare to doze off or be seen restlessly moving a leg to and fro, for the sounds about to issue from the instruments of Tansen were designed to carry the soul heavenward. It was a solemn and truly majestic occasion, and required, as Nada liked to say, "full mind."

"Then Tansen singing," Nada said, and he flung his rotund torso back and forth, closed his eyes in mock rapture, and shook his arms; he was imitating the response of the audience when this magician sang.

Apparently, they got a bit carried away by the music, and felt impelled by that thing that Louie Armstrong said was essential to swing.

King Akbar, however, didn't agree. He didn't approve of outwardly displayed enthusiasm. Individual seizures of delight were verboten.

"What is the meaning of this?" a dignified minister asked the King.

"I'll tell you tomorrow, at the next program," the King replied, in response to the murmurs of discontent. The singing ended; Akbar departed and the high-spirited crowd of music lovers dispersed.

In the meantime the King sent out a decree regarding the musical recital for the next day: "Anyone shaking or moving during the performance *will be hanged.*"

I looked aghast at Nada when he spoke of this extreme measure taken by the music-loving sovereign.

"Would you really want to hang somebody if she clapped when you were coming super-correct at triple time?" This was a serious question.

"And King before," Nada tried to explain, "no government, no regulations, whatever he say—whole world do. King full power. 'Anyone shaking—you die!' King-order—no any doubt!"

Pity an inept musician who had to perform before such a touchy tyrant.

"Next day Tansen singing again—all audience stone!"

Enthusiasm, quelled under pain of death.

"But Tansen unhappy—'What is this today?' Why all people like stone?"

Nada sat up straight and stiffened his face, miming the stone-sober audience.

"Yesterday, everybody, 'Wow! Wow!' Today nothing, all dead-face? Tansen very feel. More than ten thousand people there—only five go 'Wow!'"

It was not clear from what Nada said what the fate of the five forgetful wow-ers was. I can only hope that King Akbar did not stick to his barbarous decree. In any event, the story shows that at least five people out of the audience of ten thousand *really* liked Tansen's music.

Nada went on to defend the king's deadly decree on grounds that Tansen's music was "not earth music," and consequently should not be treated like ordinary entertainment. I could see that Nada was smarting from his own experience. But the idea of killing somebody for such a trifle is insane. The night before, a girl decided to sprawl out on her back during Nada's group class. This was an insult, he said, not to him but to God. (On the other hand, I always thought God was in the business of forgiving sinners.) For Nada, the wrong gesture, the wrong attitude put you at odds with the great powers he sensed were present in his ragas. Coming correct was not just a matter of life and death; it meant incurring the risk of reincarnating during the Kali Yuga.

From this Nada moved to a short homily on karma. This was the sum of it, in vintage Nada-rap: "Good doing, good getting; bad doing, bad getting." To illustrate his meaning he used photography as an example. Parvati, he said, always took careful photographs; the result was good photography. Others, less careful, got lopsided pictures, with feet or head missing! The result of the defective attention was a "zero" photograph. Nada drew on everyday things to spell out the wisdom of the sacred songs he learned by heart.

I tried to argue that the dance was also a vehicle of worship, and that spontaneous movement had its place and should be tolerated and maybe lauded. Nada said he wasn't criticizing anybody. His point was philosophical. Movement without understanding was mere nature, like energy without aim, like vital force without soul or insight. He understood that the girl's back was hurting. She should have moved and leaned against some wall. He was accustomed in India to certain rules, generally accepted by most people, a culture where all is ordered around the divine, so the right posture was important. To King Akbar, it was fatally crucial; it was no big deal in crazy democratic New York City.

"In India, rules. Ladies, one part; gents, one part. Ladies and gents together never sitting there. Any foreigners come, not know custom."

Parvati remarked that when she was in India she stumbled into the wrong place on more than one occasion, to her embarrassment.

"What is the meaning behind this custom of separating man and woman?" I asked.

"You see, in India lady called mother. Ladies, not ordinary—mother! All ladies mother."

"Ladies," according to Swami Nada, are not ordinary reality but manifestations of mother-shakti energy. They are too powerful, I took him to mean, to be allowed to live their own spontaneous lives. They may be archetypes but need to remain under control. Nada went on to make the point that in India—barring the nefarious Western influence of recent times—women are married once. No escape. "In India everywhere you go, all ladies called *mother.*" Every woman is viewed as an embodiment of the nurturing principle of the universe. I'm not sure I would be comfortable with that assignment, if I were a woman. Nada of course was speaking of an ideal, not of the way women are treated in the real modern India in the big cities.

"Swamiji," Parvati asked, "is this true with the Muslims?"

"Muslim, everything opposite," he said. They write from left to right, brother and sister marry; wash from feet up to face instead of from face down to feet. Everyone but Muslims are called infidel. But then he quickly drew back from these grossly slanted remarks.

"But this is not criticism," he said. "I told Parvati (he looked sharply at me)—*never criticize.* Why criticize a dream?—No, never, it comes and goes, all, a dream." He looked at Parvati, and said, smiling, "Never criticize—except when teaching music."

6

Reluctant Sannyasi

NADA WAS ROPED INTO BECOMING A MONK by Swami Sivananda, eager to build and enrich the Divine Life Society he had founded by bringing in such a gifted and well-regarded musician.

"After the kingdom was lost, you became *sannyasi*—yet you never really wanted to." The term refers to one's renunication of material possessions and one's worldly social relations.

"No, I never wanted sannyasi. And I told Parvati: never become sannyasi."

"Is becoming sannyasi a matter of taking a vow?"

"Sannyasi is an inner attitude, but should be visible in the way they live." Parvati said.

"Rules," Nada said, "sannyasi. Ninety-nine percent not do. Very difficult. How many people taking sannyasi—then, getting married. Here, easy doing no rules; in India—danger, they kill people."

These we call terrorists or psychotic fundamentalists or religious psychopaths, I think to myself.

"Twelve million sannyasi in India," Nada continues with his critique: "Everybody help sannyasi. Free food, free staying, free everything. Serve—but anything wrong doing—killing him!" There are lots of pseudo-monks capitalizing on the good will of ordinary people; but these ordinary people can also turn into killers if you upset them for some holy reason.

Nada was concerned that I know he was not at all like the typical person in the orange garb.

"I am sannyasi—I am beggar—give me, help me. . . . No, not me! I never ask donation; I teaching. My work is always singing and playing, all day and night. I not sitting silent, doing nothing, I not beggar."

"He never wanted to be a swami," Parvati said, "but Sivananda used to try to make people be swamis. Sivananda was quick to grant Swami status to wayfarers that strayed on his path. But most of the them gave it up on account of it being so hard—soon they would return to their homes."

"Many like that in India—here too," Nada said, and gave as an example a young American swami who married a certain nubile devotee of the ashram he had been presiding over. This, according to Nada, was "very bad karma." I mentioned that the same thing was widespread in the Christian church. Priests were dropping their sacerdotal robes and leaping into secular love nests at warp speed.

"Sannyasi in India never marriage, never touch ladies, never go to market. . . . Many ask: 'Make me sannyasi.' I have power; but not using. Never. I always agonist. You never come sannyasi, I say."

"Well, this is certainly realistic—and honest. No use biting off more than you can chew," I said.

"I free in Rishikesh with Sivananda. Others—two, three days— coming sannyasi." I wasn't sure what this meant other than he didn't approve of suddenly becoming a monk, given the gravity of the decision.

"What sort of a man was Swami Sivananda?" I asked.

"He, you see, was a civil surgeon. Wife, one son. Many people poor—all life, he give, give, give. He in bed, sleeping—people come, he gets up and gives!"

"They used to call him 'give-ananda,'" Parvati added.

"Once in Malaysia, before he was a swami, he purchased fifty blankets. He gave all this to people without cloth. His wife got very angry, and complained: 'Any money coming, and you give, always give it away!'"

Sivananda had stated that his father never gave him money. His father educated him—and left money matters to God and Sivananda's ingenuity. In like manner, Sivananda said he would educate his son, and provide him and his wife with the necessities of life; but beyond that he was free to dispose of his goods according to his own wishes.

"And she very angry; always fighting. 'If you die, what will happen to us?'" His wife felt insecure in the presence of Sivananda's unlimited will to serve the indigent. And then this domestic squabble:

"One day Swami Sivananda at work in hospital. She, wife, catch son; lock him in room, hold him very tight. Then out comes kerosene, start fire!"

"She burned herself and her son?" I asked, amazed to hear about the saint hassling with a crazy wife.

"Yes, very angry. When fire, cry—neighbor people came to see."

"Neighbor-people heard?" I asked.

"Yes, you see, house to house together. One thin wall separate. Each wall together doing, expense share. Call! Everybody coming. So, neighbor hear, cry. Come—door lock, break. Clothing burn." The crazy mom and kid survived.

"What happened to Sivananda and his wife?" I inquired.

"She, six months hospital. Even then, even after—Swamiji and wife fighting," Nada ruefully observed.

"After?" Parvati and I asked, astonished that even near immolation failed to stop them from bickering.

"Yes, after," Nada said with solemn emphasis, his face lighting up with roguish amusement, "fighting *even in hospital*!" Pausing philosophically, he added, "Then left—come very tired. Also resign job—people liked him there, but he resign."

He resigned his job and left his wife. The government of Malaysia allowed him to remain in the country for three months, after which he returned to India, wifeless and jobless, a mendicant. The last outpost for escapees from the woes of mundane reality.

"What did he do now?" I asked.

"He just went up. There nobody. Himalayas, empty then. He came to one ashram, a beggar."

Sannyasi. Some are just outcasts from family life, unable to tolerate the burdens of ordinary existence. They flee to the mountains, renounce everything (they have little to begin with), and surrender to the divine. That was the plan. Sivananda began to draw a following. People were attracted to him for his generosity and open spirit, and he also made himself useful by dispensing medical services; he was, after all, a physician. Finally, he had to put a sign on his door for visiting hours. He continued to dispense free medical care, gave lectures, and conducted religious chanting. More and more people gathered around him, a growing scene of spiritual light and good will.

However, a free and generous spirit can be unpredictable. "People at that ashram coming angry with Sivananda." First his wife, now the people who ran his ashram. All the attention was on Sivananda; he gave so much and was so likable that the brightness of individuals around him was eclipsed. Once Sivananda went to Pakistan where, chanting and dancing, he entertained the queen of England. The queen and other English gentlemen of quality were duly inspired by the god-intoxicated Hindu. However, in the meantime, back in the Himalayas at his ashram, two of his closest disciples were assaulted and beaten in the dead of night by hooded figures dressed in black. The beaten were laid up in the hospital for more than two months. The assailants were never identified but it seemed plain to Nada that these were ashram people.

"After fifteen days Swamiji came, the people all in bandage. 'What is this?'"

So, Swami Sivananda found himself obliged to move on to another ashram in the area of Rishikesh. This time he concentrated on being anonymous, and tried to get lost in the crowd of sannyasis. One day a spiritually minded maharaja came looking for him, came right up to Sivananda and asked: "Where is Swami Sivananda?"

"I don't know," he replied, "I am looking for him myself." Nada explained that Sivananda was afraid of more trouble and had resolved to disappear from the world of names and form. In the end, however, the maharaja discovered the identity of the elusive Swami and offered to give him some forest and rough quarters to build his own ashram. Sivananda accepted. From these humble beginnings his ashram in Rishikesh grew into the large and complex spiritual center it is today—a "city," as Nada described it.

A few days before September 8, 1953—Nada had been with Sivananda in his new ashram for three years—the musician was called before Sivananda.

"Bassaraja—tomorrow you fast," Nada was told. At that time, before he acquired his spiritual name, he was called Bassaraja.

"Why fast?" said Bassaraja, uneasily.

"You shall be made sannyasi on my birthday, September 8," said Sivananda.

"No, I not fast," he said, and indeed the next day he did not fast.

Nada explained that these were the rules one followed in becoming sannyasi; a fast day prior to the ceremony. But Nada had no wish to become a monk; anyway, Sivananda never before conducted this ceremony on his birthday. So Nada made it a point not to fast and ate something. Sivananda, laughing, kept insisting he was going to make Nada over into a monk.

"Everyday I practice, early morning. That morning, barber call. I practice—and door—knock, knock. 'What is this?' I think. 'Who is this?' No one ever comes that way, that time, no one ever knocks on my door. I silent. 'Who are you?'"

Nada's face assumed a look of amazed trepidation. They were coming to enforce upon him a marriage vow. It happened once before when he was a young man who knew his own mind and wanted to be free. His parents wanted to tie Nada up in the knot called marriage. So now again, after many years lord of himself, the cunning of fate was prodding him to take another, different kind of marriage vow.

"Swami Sivananda calls you," replied the barber.

"Why so early?" cries out Nada.

"Swami Sivananda calls you," sounded the fateful refrain.

"And after, birthday program starting," Nada said. Apparently, having eaten, and despite the ominous appearance of the barber, Bassaraja still didn't think anything too grave was about to happen.

"Very nice birthday program. Swami Sivananda laughing; I laughing. Still laughing everybody, suddenly, four people holding me!"

Nada made a hilarious gesture describing the action of a razor that left him the glossy-headed sannyasi.

"Was Swami Sivananda watching?" Parvati wanted to know.

"Yes," said Nada, "force, hold me, those four. Barber cut. Swamiji watching and laughing!

"I don't want sannyasi," Nada pleaded.

Sivananda, who was a giant of a man, just leaned back and enjoyed the funny spectacle. Nada explained that Sivananda's objective in doing this was to protect him from continued family abuse. Once the musician became a monk, he could stay unhindered at the ashram, which is what he wanted in the first place. To escape the bonds of family life, he became a monk; but in his heart of hearts, Nada chafed at the bonds of religious life. All family life is the same, too much bickering and too much restraint of the free spirit, he argued. Nada chose the least of the evils: what allowed him the greatest freedom from distraction. Turning into a monk would enable him to nurse his passion to make music.

"So they stole your hair?" I said, commenting on Nada's abduction into religious life.

"Catch me!—Four people. Barber catch my feet. What can I do? Swamiji ordered! I told them, 'Don't touch me! Don't touch me!' And everyone there laughing, all laughing. What can I do?" Nada smiled as he told this story; his voice dramatically expressive of amused resignation.

"Everybody doing *namaskari*—many people crying that day."

"Happy or unhappy?" I asked.

"I do not know," he replied. "But after that, I follow rule. Swami Sivananda told me how going and coming in this world: I follow, serve, love, give, never come angry, never think anything. From that day—never think! Never plan—why plan? He, you know, God, is the Driver. I never plan."

"When you plan, you have to program yourself. Too much work," Parvati added in full agreement with her teacher, or, as she put it to me, "her best friend."

"I never giving sannyasi in my life. I have got power, but never. Many people ask, every year—but I silent. Why?" His explanation was that the people who approached him were naïve and more whimsical than spiritual. "Many sannyasi—talking, talking—but not practicing. Talking good, not being good?"

I remarked that it was time for Swamiji's walk; and time for me to go. He smiled and said: "I never thinking time. I thank you anyway for your time, for your giving yourself." I bowed to my gracious teacher and stepped out on to West 24th Street, where I was greeted by a chaotic wave of New York City noise that caused me to quicken my step, laughing to myself as I thought of Nada being forced into becoming a monk as an alternative to family, work, and the oppressive responsibilities of ordinary life, all of which hindered his one great need, which was *to make music*. And to make music *divine*.

7

Krishna's Flute

"SWAMIJI," I SAID, THE MOMENT I sat down beside him on this April day, "I want to ask you a question. You say the flute is only entertainment—but why do you always see Krishna with a flute? Krishna is always playing a flute; it must be more than just entertainment."

It seemed to me that a flute or any instrument—tin harmonica or Irish pennywhistle—could become an instrument for making sacred sound and losing yourself in it. I was curious to hear his reply.

He looked up at me without hesitation and said, "This is a god, yes, true, Krishna is always with flute. Once, in a forest he walked. There Lord Krishna found a simple piece of bamboo, hollow and ordinary, nothing very beautiful, nothing. . . ."

Parvati, silent and self-contained, glided in, laid some coffee at the feet of Nada, and disappeared.

"I take some coffee now," he said, and added with robust contentment: "I never thinking of getting, or of coming and going—I ask . . . I ask God."

Nada didn't just see Parvati hand him a cup of coffee. He saw the unfolding of the divine will, the incarnation of his morning prayers. It was the way he saw the world, in one sense impersonal, but in another, poetic. And at bottom, practical. I tried to be as attentive as I could to the ideas and images that came out of the monk-musician. There had to be a link between Nada's picture of reality and the extraordinary man that he became. He sipped his coffee.

"You see, I'll tell you," Nada resumed about the flute, "Lord Krishna took that one bamboo from the forest and made *murali*, six holes. *Kama, krodha, moha*—right hand—*lobha, mada, matsara*—left hand. Six habits everybody have. Kama—everybody have. . . ."

"Kama means desire?" I said, remembering the Kama Sutra.

"Love, you know, ladies and gents. Ladies want man. Man want ladies. This is called kama. But this kama you keep for God. Your kama is used there."

A handy instrument to have around—this flute of Krishna! Use it to escape the hassles of romantic love and turn human desire into divine consciousness. Easier said than done. Music for Nada was serious emotional alchemy. The art of sublimating the rubbish of experience into gold.

"Krodha," he continued, "is everybody coming angry. Not getting success, coming angry. You angry, yes? That also use for God."

"Use the anger to seek God?" I said.

"God everything." He replied.

Then he went back to kama. "You want girl?—yes?" he said almost quizzically.

"Oh yeah," I nodded.

"Nature, animals also, but this kama you use for God. And krodha same, use anger for God. And moha, moha means you want everything for self."

"Greed, possessiveness."

"But now you want same but . . ."

"I see," I said. "Better to be greedy for God than for money, power, and fame."

He gave me a low humming sound of approval.

"Not seven or eight holes in murali, six, everybody have six habits. In beginning, Lord Krishna start this murali. Murali means your mind."

"Well," I said, "I see where you're going with this." The man had a one-track mind—but what a track! Convert every drop of experience into God consciousness.

"This is very good meaning of that flute. Meaning? Not ordinary!" Nada said with childlike enthusiasm. "Kama, krodha, moha. . . ."

"That's on the right hand," I said. "what about the left?"

He started to say lobha, hesitated, went back to the beginning, counting on his fingers, kama, krodha, moha, and then adding rapidly, lobha, mada, matsara."

"What is lobha?" I asked, eager to proceed.

He went on a bit, listing the habits and passions of humankind we can use to transform ourselves.

"And moha—I want, I want—but now—I want God, I want God." He seemed then to wander into another metaphor.

"Now, child come, bringing nothing, God give us everything. First, girl, no milk; nine months finish, milk coming. God make arrangement for milk coming!" he said, his eyes sparkling with wonder. It was obvious that for Nada no biological description would account for the mystery of mammary glands. Nada's worldview, pre-scientific and mythical, was to trace all things back to the first Cause; at all times to yield to the all-embracing bosom of the Divine Being.

"Why no coming milk with man?" he queried, lingering on this graphic exemplar of the divine process. "Everything God give us. So, whatever you have, give!"

He wanted to show me the moon rock that one of the astronauts had given him. When he first told me the story of the moon rock it was to illustrate the decadence of our age. In the Kali Yuga, men need rockets to fetch a few stones from the lunar surface; but in earlier ages when men were really powerful and in touch with "Truth," they could just teleport to the moon, and get all the rocks they wanted.

He told me a story about a visit he had with the president of General Motors. The yogin from Rishikesh was given a tour of the assembly line and allowed to witness the magic of capitalism in all its harrowing glory.

"Sitting at round table, all telephone, talking all country. There I sat, half hour waiting, many busy men coming, going, no room there but trucks and cars and wheels, and we are waiting."

"'I sorry, Swamiji,' he say, 'very busy.' Each minute car going out. Many design, many things to do—trucks and motors, and this and that, always something. . . .'" Nada fully understood the source of all this busyness, so he said: "Yes, I see—one second very costly. Then I ask him: 'How much income you getting?' His answer: 'One hour, six million dollars.'

"I tell him, not enough!"

I laughed out loud thinking of the look on the CEO's face. But then Nada hit the CEO hard, and said: "One day die, not bring anything, not one penny. So what is your aim? What is your life? He is surprised by my question." Nada paused, then continued: "How you come, you go—empty. Not going special place—Ford manager—everybody same place—cemetery." The cemetery was Nada's beloved rhetorical grenade.

He liked to hammer this mantra home: "King also going, president also going, billionaire also going—and beggar also going."

"'What can I do?' Big Ford manager say. He very feel. He starts to cry. And then I give him mantra: Everything come from God—gold, diamonds, food, drink—morning give thanks, night before sleep, take God's name. I show you letter. He changed, yes, change was real, chanting now and everything."

Several times Nada Brahmananda told me of encounters with various CEOs in America who paused to engage with him. In one story, he reduced another important captain of capitalism to tears and sincere acts of contrition. The ghandarva's brief travels in America did not lead to the overthrow of plutocracy or the end of consumerism. Nevertheless, wherever he went he left a trail of powerful psychic effects, pointing to the nullity of everything except the music of transcendence.

Far from losing steam that afternoon, he went on with his musings. I heard him say, summing things up: "Always fighting, if you think. Always happiness, if you love—this is Prema." I could see his point. And cheers for Prema. Then he quoted Kabir, coming back to one of his favorites: "*Khali ana khala jana.*" Nada never tired of quoting these few words, the essence of his world-view, emptiness. "Empty coming, empty going." That was Nada's point of departure for thinking about life and the world. There was a connection between emptiness and the flute. The flute is an empty tube in the way a human life is an open vehicle for the spirit of life to flow through. Without breath and spirit, we die—and we *stop the music.*

"King, not bring kingdom, millionaire, not bring one penny. Whatever you have, serve—not serve, what you getting? Pig! Mud-eating. . . ."

He peered at me very seriously and asked: "Pig you have seen?"

"Yes," I replied.

"Here very clean. In India very dirty, mud, mud everywhere. There pig sleeping!"

His remarks on pigs and mud were evidently based on experience. I could see that the former court musician of the King of Mysore had a real horror of pigs, and when he warned against failing to obtain moksha and coming back on a fresh round of rebirths he was thinking of reincarnating as a mud-wallowing pig.

"Yes, sleeping and eating in mud. Why? Pig not helping anyone. This is punishment. You eat mud."

"But Nada," I said, "that's not true and not kind to the pig. The pig does serve humans—in fact, he's *served up* to humans. The pig, actually a fairly smart animal, becomes tasty pork chops and is regularly sacrificed to the pig-loving appetites of humans." But eating pork was unknown to the nada yogi who once proudly invited me to scrutinize his teeth. He wanted me to know that he used them mainly for making sounds and not ever for masticating fish, flesh, or fowl.

Again he launched into a litany of declarations on the emptiness of everything, his voice evoking the melancholy passage of time, the play of atoms and the void, the waning of epochs, the futility of all our dreams. His voice was his magic, and I felt a curious blend of exultation and melancholy, serenity and despair, blended while listening to him. His Kaliesque worldview, so relentlessly grim, somehow became soothing, as he worked it into my musical self.

Suddenly, he remarked: "Animals better than us—you show me animal smoking, drinking whiskey, buying, stealing. But in nature, no income tax, no city tax, no police, no court—all better than us!"

The case for the "better" character of the natural world and against the exploitations of nature by humans is much clearer today, being told by real experts that we have about a decade to stave off the crash of world civilization. Nada went back to his theme of human contentiousness, which he recalled from Sivananda's endless bickering with his wife.

"Why is man always fighting?" I asked.

"Always fighting!" he answered, not answering, and clapped his hands. But then he thought a moment and said: "Everybody own self-love—own self-love," he said, echoing himself. Nada never said something only once but liked to repeat an idea the way he would repeat a musical riff. He never thought in linear order but in images that duplicated themselves and rhythmic patterns that kept changing their tempo.

He lingered a while longer on the theme of the superiority of animals, pointing out that they never ate the bad foods we do (no longer true), and stressing how all-important the right food was. Then he came back and said: "Yes, kama, krodha, moha. And Mada—ego! I am everything! I am great! I am beautiful! I am wonderful! Yah! Yah! Use that too—you see, use Krishna-flute, and man-ego becoming God-ego. Now you are singing, playing flute in forest, in street, in latrine! Everywhere playing—I am everything! I am beautiful! I am wonderful! Yes, yes, very true—but who is this 'I?'"

We have all the material we need to realize the hidden mystery of our being. The paradox is that this fullness is a kind of emptiness. We alone can produce harmony out of ourselves, a oneness from the chaos. Who else? Nada's philosophy refused to do violence to any human emotion. Every ache of longing, every pang of resentment, every swaggering ambition was usable: the messy whole of our existence, no matter how uncertain or unpromising, is the matrix of our self-discovery.

"And now matsara," he said, coming to the end of the catalogue, "criticize—people always criticize. Why do it? Waste! Waste! Nothing getting."

"Instead criticize yourself, work on yourself," I said, thinking this was the next point he was going to make.

He made a face that seemed to indicate approval but then added: "Not too much, not too much—but smooth and lovely. And never think bad, Michael—understanding first, then all good coming automatically."

I recalled the esoteric etymology of Nada's name about the "union of breath and fire of intellect," and thought how much the name matched the man. Despite his nonlinear, nonliterate background, sovereign intellect was the root of all with Swamiji.

"All these six habits, you use. And so Lord Krishna plays the flute and gives blessings, very good sound, and all girls and rishis, elephants and snakes and tigers, all forest beings enjoy! And inside that bamboo flute, look! What do you see? Empty!"

With that his hand came down on the harmonium and he struck a plaintive chord. Then he handed me his old book of ragas. He turned to the last page and showed it to me.

"How many ragas?" he asked.

"Four hundred and fifty," I replied.

"Yes," he said, and began in a low voice to read them one by one: "*Bhairavi, bhupa, malakauns, yaman . . .*" his voice trailing off, as the divine songman mused on the tools of his trade.

"Never look at book. I all in," he said, and explained how the various ragas belonged to the seasons and also the phases of day and night. All the archetypes of existence are contained in these age-old ragas.

"Timing, timing, all is timing," he said, and chanted a few phrases from a song in the mode of raga Malakauns.

"When Lord Krishna start singing this one," he stopped abruptly, commenting on what he had just sung, "everybody wonder, 'What is this song?' Any worker there working—stop. . . ."

He was translating. Before long I realized it was impossible, and beside the point, to sort out what Nada really believed and thought and what was being quoted from the song. His mind had long ago threaded its way into the tapestry of his tradition. I was content to sit at the seashore, listening to waves breaking, knowing they had their beginnings in the ocean of Nada's spiritual raga world. He became silent and then mused on Krishna's magic flute. "And any snake there—stop and stand. Cow stand. Tiger stand. Man stand. Everybody stand."

Then on to another raga about music magic: "One time there by the holy river a girl was carrying water—she working, but all of a sudden stop. 'Where is she?' everyone ask. She's gone. Girl say: 'My mind— He take.'"

So the flute of Lord Krishna stole the working-girl's mind, stopping her workaday world, and stopping the cow and the snake and the tiger in their worlds, too.

"And Lord Krishna stay there by the river, called Jamuna" said the translator of sea wisdom and wind wisdom. And again he sang, and Nada's soul-husky voice took *my* mind away."When I taking water, I forget," Nada said, still with the girl's raga mind, and resumed singing, then paused again: "How can I go home now without water—what will my mother say? What say my husband?"

The power of Krishna's flute was beginning to dawn on me. "Swamiji," I said, "if everybody listens to Krishna's flute, all life will end in the forest, husband and wife will part, the world as we know it will stop and probably fall to pieces."

He looked up at me sharply and began to speak when Parvati came in and said something about an errand she had just performed. They exchanged some talk about lawyers; it was apparently a matter of some concern. Parvati looked pale, a glint of testiness in her eyes. She was hankering to retreat to her incense-suffused little room, but duty made her go on many jaunts around Manhattan.

Nada smiled at his lovely disciple, sang a few mata of the song, and asked her in a schoolmasterly fashion: "What is this raga?"

"Raga Malakauns," she said, her face softening into a radiant smile.

"Correct," said the master, sighing with satisfaction. He indicated to me with a glance that the lesson was over. The ghandarva had to attend to some annoyingly mundane matters. As for my lesson, I gained a marvelous, new understanding of my flute. It was a liberating insight, and I thought to myself: Any art form may be viewed as a spiritual practice, and in the end, life itself is the great sadhana.

8

A Gift from an Old Man

NADA WAS DRILLING ME ON THE CHANT that began *jaya guru dev jaya* . . . praise the angelic teacher who is a messenger from beyond. He said this was a song with a universal message, praising the lords that transmit the one light of being, the single source of life-enhancing spirit. In the chant, *guru deva* becomes Eso Christos, and gets four beats in tal keherawa, just as Hanumana and Sita Ram get four beats, and all the other lords and buddhas, warriors and apostles.

We paused a moment and he offered me some water that I gladly drank. The late afternoon was sultry and oppressive. I stretched my legs and mentioned that I would like to get a set of tabla but couldn't afford to. Silently, he took my arm and began drumming on my skin. My dream came back—a music lesson with no instrument—my body was the instrument.

"No need for drum," he said, as he drummed on my body. My body was the drum, anywhere was a place to practice, anything was an instrument, omnipresent were the means to the true inner music.

"One two, one two . . ." he tapped on me, looking straight into my eyes and laughing, "nothing special, easy, balance. You practice—*do . . . it . . . now.*" He pronounced the latter three words slowly and distinctly.

Nada reached over suddenly and got his icon of Siva—the one he gazes at when he does *nadakhumbaka* every morning at three o'clock.

"I tell you history of this now." Nada chose that moment to narrate the story of his strange icon. It was a silver framed case that opened with two images. The image on the left depicted the entranced and epicene persona of Krishna, and a serpentine form spelling out a sacred syllable floating around his head. At the bottom on the left the letters D. I. N. were written in Roman script and, on the right, the letters K. I. V. D. I. N. stood for "Do It Now"—a motto of the Divine Life Society. Nada interpreted K. I. V. to mean "Keep It in View." I saw now why he decided to tell me about the icon. I got the idea of drumming, then he said *do it now*, when it seemed I was ready to let my idea of drumming languish in the limbo of mere possibility, dependent on buying a new drum.

The secret of maintaining the correct attitude, the keen and lithe readiness to translate idea into action, was to keep the vision in view and in focus. This was the purpose of the icon—a visible image that speaks directly to the self and stirs the wellsprings of one's spiritual energy. The image on the right-hand side of the silver case showed a trident with a circle and eyes surrounding it. The eyes are open and gaze, clear and pitiless, upon the world. Before the trident, which is mounted on three steps, a lion in motion is pictured. This is the image of Siva, the dancing god of destruction and liberation—the fierce gaze of concentration that cuts like diamond through the fog of human ignorance. It was a striking icon to contemplate.

"This picture is called *murti* and means 'temple.' Doing nadakhumbaka, I always keep this picture before me."

"It helps the concentration?"

"Yes. My eyes always see face of Lord Siva sitting there. I do not think this is just a picture. I think Lord Siva sitting there—not piece of paper. Real sitting Lord Siva. I look, eyes not blinking; mind always thinking Lord Siva. Meantime, hands doing tabla. This is meditation."

He clapped his hands and counted, pretending he was drumming.

"*Nadhidhina*, nadhidhina . . . breath holding five minutes, ten minutes, thirty minutes, death-body coming . . . my mind always meditating on Lord Siva."

"How did you get this murti?" Parvati asked.

"It was in Ghoati, Ceylon, 1961. Very big city—and big program."

Nada explained that there were many rich and lazy Indians in Ceylon at that time; they had a monopoly on all the means to wealth, and the government sided with the capitalist elite. The exploited natives accordingly rose up in protest, burning the cars of the big business men and looting the shops. When the furor died down, there was a big program that featured the celestial songman, Nada Brahmananda.

"After program everybody come on platform and catch my hand. Namaskar! Wonderful! Wonderful! And then one old man come."

"After you did the *khumbaka* this happened?"

"Yes," Nada replied. "'Swamiji, maharaj,' old man say, 'this is my humble gift to you.' He give me murti, and I take it. And I look, picture of Lord Siva."

Nada picked up the murti, placed it over his eyes, and bowed, showing what he did when the old man gave him the gift. He removed the murti from his eyes.

"One second pass—'thank you, namaskara,' I say—gone that old man, gone! I look everywhere but gone! I ask, 'Where is he?' Many people on platform catch my hand and feet. No one see—and that old man gone! Very lovely murti—like that I never saw."

"Are you sure no one else saw the old man on the platform?"

"Nobody saw."

Parvati enquired: "Was it Lord Siva who came down to give you the murti?"

"Yes," he said instantly with a tone of, *How could you doubt it?* "Lord Siva signature," he said matter-of-factly.

Parvati and I laughed heartily at this. Not that we doubted Swamiji's story, but it did seem a little remarkable that Lord Siva should put his signature on his picture.

"What does this trident symbolize?" I asked. The trident is a symbol of Siva; I was curious how Nada viewed it.

"Any trouble coming," he answered promptly, "kill him!" Okay, after all, it did look like a weapon. I felt sure the trident also was meant to signify the power to cut through the fog and falsehoods that typically permeate so much of established life. Nada went on to say the trident symbolized the three *gunas,* which are forces or modes of being: *sattva* (mental clarity), *rajas* (emotional intensity), and *tamas* (obtuse sluggishness). Siva had all the gunas under control.

"So," I said, "you really believe this murti came from Siva?"

Parvati was examining the murti and said, "Look here, there *are* signatures, one under each picture."

"Signatures?" I remarked.

"Yes, Siva," Nada put in, unable to abandon his theory of the origin of the murti.

But Parvati, more sober, observed: "This means some artist painted them."

But this by itself did not rule out the possibility of the murti's paranormal appearance from the old man that nobody saw but Nada.

"You know," I said, "Sai Baba apparently materializes objects that look very commercial. Do you know Sai Baba, Swamiji?"

"Yes, he came to our ashram in 1955. Very thin boy then. No big hair like now."

He was alluding to Sai Baba's rather spectacular hairdo. Sai Baba was on his way to Badrinas, three hundred miles north, very high in the Himalayas, a place where Lord Vishnu stayed and practiced great austerities. People go there to bathe in the hot springs, flanked by the snowy fastness. In former times pilgrims had to walk for six months to reach this remote sanctuary. Now it was much easier; roads and buses were available.

"Sai Baba is very famous for miracles, Swamiji—did you ever notice him do anything strange?"

"Yes," Nada replied and described the materialization of sacred beads that he had witnessed. This was one type of Sai Baba's reported miraculous doings.[1]

"You believe this is real, Swamiji?"

"Yes," he said with urgency, "this is *siddhi,* power; music is my power."

Even the miraculous powers called siddhis come from practice—from focusing attention on a given task.

"If I love and serve you long time," Nada clarified, "I receive something. Must."

He then recounted a tale of an Indian saint who inhabited a dry desert region for a long time, performed severe *tapas,* or austerities, out of which came the creation of a fountain of fresh water. Thanks to these saintly exertions, many a wayfarer of the desert was saved from dying of thirst. And one thinks of Bernadette Soubirous, the Virgin Mary visionary who dug up with her hands a spring of water in a Lourdes garbage dump that became the scene of a famous healing shrine.

Nada followed with another story of another saint who haunted a barren wilderness where he practiced austerities. Once, it seems, a king with his army came by and they were in need of food. "One million people food cooking not easy," Nada said, his voice rising to a pitch of great earnestness. "Everybody, all military, come and take lunch. And nothing, nothing there—one small hut, no cooking pots. After one hour, lunch ready for million people! Everyone there very surprise."

I couldn't refrain from laughing a little, thinking about this sudden preparation of lunch for a million people in a small hut with no cooking utensils. Was I supposed to take that claim seriously? Swami Nada looked at me quizzically.

"I'll show you; that place called Anigonda. After one hour, food was ready—people never eat like that before! That was this saint's power—his name Jamadagne." Whether meant as history or mythology, to Nada, it wasn't a distinction that made a difference. Still, I decided to press the point. I knew stories of the paranormal creation of food in the Bible and in accounts of saints of various traditions.

"Swamiji, is this story real—or only story?"

"Real," was his unhesitating response. "Before, everybody have this power."

"What happened then? Why so little power now?"

"Working week, getting money—working, working. Tapas then."

"They did a lot of penance and austerity for these powers," Parvati remarked.

The talk turned to people who specialized in *mantra siddhis*. Here the power resulted from an esoteric manipulation of sound-formulas.

"Saint giving mantra—no need to eat or sleep one year. Another mantra: poison not hurt, fire not harm. No pain also. I saw."

There are Christian groups that handle poisonous snakes and drink kerosene to demonstrate the power of faith, not without the occasional fatality. There are pain-defying performances, more in a scientific spirit; Jack Schwartz, for instance, under controlled conditions at the Menninger Foundation in Topeka, Kansas, pushed an unsterilized darning needle through his biceps. There was no bleeding nor did the monitoring equipment register any physiological response. Schwartz did this repeatedly and never showed pain or got infected. The book *Arigo: The Surgeon With A Rusty Knife,* by John G. Fuller, is a powerful challenge to anyone with fixed ideas about what is humanly possible.

As for mantras that eliminate the need for nutrition for a year, the comparison that comes to mind would be with the Catholic visionary and stigmatic of Konnersreuth, Therese Neumann. According to witnesses and investigators, this rather plump lady nourished herself for the last thirty-five years of her life exclusively on the Holy Eucharist (a thin wafer). She was quite hardy and cheerful, got around in various public venues, was regularly exposed to the public eye, but was never seen to eat, drink, sneak a snack, or use a toilet for natural purposes.

"Are there still such mantra siddhi people around?"

"Yes, few though—and not teaching. Secret. Rules giving—not follow, very dangerous!"

"I don't understand."

"These people with mantra power have certain rules," Parvati said, "for example, wherever they are, outdoors or in a room, they have to have some water with them."

"Parvati," Nada said, "I'll show you in India one man, Chandradas, who lived near our ashram. Thousand *bhutas* he had."

"Bhutas are ghosts, spirits," Parvati translated.

"Anything this man giving order, bhutas doing. All bhutas wait on him. One time Chandradas forget water."

Nada paused and seemed to be visualizing what he was talking about: "Big house, no lock—bhutas serve him."

"What happened when he forgot the water?"

"Killed him!" Nada clapped his hands sharply.

"The ghosts killed Chandradas," Parvati specified dryly. She unpinned her long dark hair and slowly turned her neck. She leaned back against the wall and stretched her legs out.

"Do you believe in ghosts, Swamiji?" I said.

"Yes," he replied instantly, "bhuta not see with eye, only mantra siddhi man see. Anything want, order! Hat! Thank you. Very nice."

"Yes," I agreed, "very nice as long as you don't forget the water."

"You see, I told you once: mind control is life."

"Did you yourself ever see bhutas, Swamiji?"

"No, myself no—but there!"

"I have," I mused half out-loud, "an overweight ghost with bad body odor once jumped into bed with me. Woke me up."

Parvati glanced at me and continued to question Nada: "You never saw a spirit-form like when Swami Vishnu saw the form of Sivananda when he died? Vishnu said he heard his voice, came out of the tent, and saw him—clear!"

"No, I never saw. My life is music. I do not doubt anything. I believe everything. Historical, everything!"

I noticed a curious asymmetry here; Nada never saw or thought much about ghosts but believes in them—they are even "historical." I've had direct contact with an angry ghost, but still am not sure what it was, my psychic projection or something with a will of its own.

Nada's picture of reality was not from books, modern theories, newspapers, corporate advertising, or the like. I was glad to engage with a mind evolved from the archetypal Indian imagination tested by millennia of human experience. To think, breathe, and exist mythically, as I understood was the case with Nada, was in stark contrast with tradition-less modern "man," uncertain of his own nature or capacities. Nada's teachings pointed the way back to modes of thought and styles of being more akin to mythology than to modern cosmology.

Again Nada brought up Kali, the time-spirit that presently has us in its grip. I asked what he meant by Kali Yuga.

"Kali Yuga mean mind uncontrol. Before *satyayuga,* time when God is together with us. Eating and drinking together, man and God. Like that at first. God on Earth then."

God on Earth? What are these *yugas,* these ages of humanity? Kali Yuga—according to the Indian scholar, Alain Daniélou—refers to the age of conflicts (*kali*) and differs from Kali, the goddess of time and death.

In satyayuga no one suffers the pangs of doubt in matters of religious faith. In that age, acquaintance with God is as common as acquaintance with the blue sky or the green forest. The divine is present at the dinner table, visible in the starry sky, felt in every breath taken, heard in the words of common conversation.

"God is everywhere—but don't see. Then man saw God everywhere." This idea has the air of animism. The first Greek philosopher,

Thales, said: "All things are full of gods." No need to shout creeds or brandish belief systems. It's all a question of perception, and where you are in the cycles of cosmic time.

"Kali Yuga means bad people coming to power," Nada said, and added, "good people taken down." A critical turn is "when Lord Krishna left his body, more than five thousand years ago."

"Is Krishna real?" I asked, "or are these only stories? Did he walk the planet like Jesus?"

"Real," Nada said, his voice rising in earnest. "I'll show you everything."

He described a famous garden in India, called Vrandavan, that is locked up every night. If you go to this garden in India—and it seemed Nada was ready to take me there on the spot—at night you can hear music and the sounds of dancing within. But the garden is carefully guarded and locked down.

"Why is the garden locked?"

"God sleeping inside," he said calmly and without a hint of irony.

Nada believed in all the sacred traditions and stories. Myth was history and doubt was death. He would agree with William Blake: "If the sun and moon should doubt, they'd immediately go out." Nada believed in the myths that he sang and chanted.

"One thief wants to see inside garden," he continued, "very dark, everyone curious about God sleeping inside. In the morning thief came out. He said, 'I saw.' And then he starts to speak—but can't. Sudden, his brain all on fire, and he dies!"

The intruder in Krishna's garden of mystery was about to reveal some divine secrets but his brain burst into flame. The light of reality could not be contained by this foolish thief of the age of Kali.

"This was a real thief, Swamiji? Did you see him yourself?"

"Many people see, not I," he said with a hint of impatience in his voice.

"This is no great surprise," he said, looking at me with reproving eyes. In order to confirm the veracity of this tale of the thief who stole into Krishna's garden, he told of a miraculous lady known for her ability to transmute mud into delicious food. He himself knew of this because he'd been to the scene of the wonders and sampled some of the paranormal banquet.

"She's not there today, though," Parvati added by way of qualification, "only the place. Her name was Annasura."

"We are also taking mud; everybody take mud there," Nada said.

"You get food out of mud?" I remarked dully.

"She got!" Nada said indignantly. She had the power; that was her siddhi. Food want—anything at all—say: you getting! No fire, no pot, no cooking—ready!"

"Like Sai Baba today," Parvati said.

"This lady nothing special then—now people not doing sadhana, not doing tapas. Lazy, people lazy in Kali Yuga." The more he spoke of Kali Yuga—the dark age of humanity—the more it seemed he was describing the normal human condition.

"People have thousand tons of food—not giving, selfish. Before, not like this; anything have, serve, give. I eating, other people hungry, don't care. That is Kali Yuga,"

We fell into a silence. Well, I thought, some people do care. And some times and cultures are kinder and wiser than others. Nada looked up at me.

"Believe," he said.

"Yes, that's the secret of it all. But that's the hardest thing in Kali Yuga—no trust, no belief," I said.

He bemoaned the lack of honesty and consistency of people. "Artificial, never coming success. 'You are very nice,' I say, but inside, no love—only talking."

Nada paused; I searched his totally open face, the expression youthful and mobile; he played with his soft, baby-like, eighty-one-year-old toe. The skin of the soles of his feet was smooth and fresh.

"People before, in and out, one. Now, inside something, outside something."

A reign of hypocrisy. This seemed the final estimate of the nature of Kali Yuga, the sorry fate of the human animal at its worst, a creature doomed to duplicity and self-dividedness.

I placed the murti of Lord Siva, the gift from the mysterious old man, back where I found it. Nada remarked again that when he gazes upon the murti during nadakhumbaka, the picture of Siva comes alive and starts to move and shake.

"Everywhere I go, I take it with me."

"Which image do you look at when you meditate?"

"Both," he said, "one eye on one image, one eye on the other."

Nada rounds off the tale with the remark that no one so far had succeeded in capturing the murti on film; either nothing came out or else the image was blurred. I asked if I might try my hand at getting a shot. The next day I came by with my Pentax 35 and set the picture case on the radiator, which was near the light. It was a summer day, and quite warm, and there was no heat coming from the radiator. I took two shots very close up, each time focusing the image sharply.

I had the Tri-x Kodacolor film developed. The two shots of the murti came out but they were indeed blurred; the rest of the prints I shot from the roll were normal and clear. I showed the photographs of the murti to an acquaintance who was a professional photographer. His impression was *not* that the images were unfocussed when I shot them—they certainly seemed focused to me—but that there was a doubling of the image. He concluded that the cause was the icon. The icon, it would then seem, was vibrating in some subtle and normally inexplicable fashion. That would explain the report that others were unable to capture a clear image of the Siva icon on film.

9

Landlord contra Swami

IN THE TORPID ATMOSPHERE of the June afternoon, I ate lightly and arranged myself as often as possible into asanas—postures inviting the spirit of vitality. I stepped out of the house to catch the bus for New York City when I was greeted by the stout and deeply stationary figure of my landlord.* Normally an easy-going man, he seemed pained to ask me about who it was and how long they would be staying?

I had mentioned to my new landlord that I might have a few guests stay with me a while. I said who Nada was, and Parvati, and told a bit of his unusual story, stressing his wonderful purity and healing simplicity of soul, adding that he was a musician and master of a rare form of sound yoga. With such an introduction I thought my jittery landlord would be pacified.

"*If* they stay," I said, trying to maintain an air of casualness, "well . . . I really don't know . . . maybe a month."

Immediately, a wall of resistance sprang up. The landlord, normally congenial, was frowning uncomfortably.

"That's not good," he solemnly said, and lowered his eyes.

I had been picturing Swami Nada, in his orange sari, strolling up

---

*By this time I had moved from my apartment in Greenwich Village.

Woodlawn Avenue, pausing and playing with the children, charming
the stray dogs and cats, and maybe teaching some nervous members of
the neighborhood to play a little tabla. I was also thinking of the landlord's wife whose edginess showed up in her allergies to flowers, cats,
and dogs.

"Why is that?" I said.

"You know," he replied, pointing to the stone stairway before us,
"he's an old man and he might fall down the stairs."

I knew this morbid speculation was not born of compassion.

"You shouldn't think bad thoughts like that—besides, Swami Nada
Brahmananda is the most balanced man in the world. He could pirou-
ette on your chimney top, if you asked him to." I was hoping for a smile,
but instead he replied: "You have to see it from my point of view. If he
falls, he could sue me."

I tried to allay his fears. "The swami was a teacher on a mission
from an ashram in the Himalayas. He's here to pass on his healing wisdom to the citizens of Jersey City, and . . ."

"You know, he's probably a nice fellow . . . but I know a guy like
me who owned a house and whose son punctured a varicose vein in the
garden . . . and would you believe it?—the son sued the father!"

You could say my landlord was not given to trusting his fellow
men. Not into metanoia, he seemed to have a thing for paranoia. He
hinted that the monk would have the key and might let his friends
and family relations in, and that the entire neighborhood might soon
be swarming with Hindus and swamis. Then and there I decided I
would drop the idea, enchanting as it was, of using my apartment as a
way station for my wandering minstrel friends. Other solutions would
turn up, I was sure. On this point, I would apply Nada's wisdom of
"not thinking" and leaving it to God or, if you prefer, the gods of
Chance or the Subliminal Mind.

Starting out a bit late, I got to Manhattan on time. On 24th Street,
wading through the humid haze, I noticed Parvati in the distance; she

waved and her whole body rippled a wonderful hello. I described the incident with the landlord to her. A more congenial ashram might soon be available anyway, she said. We agreed that providence had to be on Nada's side, and parted with a soft handshake; she had errands to attend to.

At the ashram for today's lesson, we plunged into the Universal Raga, the King of Ragas, the raga that is sung in "the whole world."

Java guru dev . . . hail to the divine teacher, to Jesus and Buddha, to Aphrodite and Dionysos, and so forth, and give them all four beats in the garland of names and forms. We sang and drummed, drummed and sang, and my mind was swimming.

Singing was like swimming. Even strokes, proper breathing—then a visit from the imp of the perverse, and I imagined I was about to get a cramp—not good, if you're swimming to save your life. My mistakes on the harmonium multiplied like snakes on the head of Medusa.

"Again," he said.

I tried to explain that some bizarre inner foe was out to get me. Nada smiled and placed my hand on the harmonium. My phantoms were inconceivable abstractions to him. So, we played on, and I made so many mistakes I caused the master to make mistakes. After a while we both got strangely in tune with each other in spite of all the mistakes. We found new rhythms, improvised around our misses, and I stumbled back into coming correct. It was an unusual lesson and I learned you could make a kind of art out of your misses and mishaps, as long as you maintain the flow of your attention, and as long as you don't lose sight of what you're aiming for.

I was about to leave the ashram when Parvati appeared, and Nada said they would join me for a walk outside. I knew they were both considering the possibility of a discreet departure from the ashram. The wandering troubadours were having difficulties securing stable living quarters. It was unclear whether agents of Sivananda's Divine Life Society or Swami Vishnu's True World Order were responsible for their material needs.

I explained that the elderly people who owned the house and lived below my apartment were not against the idea of a visit. I had to say they might get rattled by the tabla at three o'clock in the morning when Nada performed nadakhumbaka. I could see Nada was distressed at the thought that he might be a disturbance. With a touch of hurt indignation, he said: "I will bring *swarmandala* and play for them. Even tigers, leopards, and cobras like music on swarmandala."

The three of us stepped out onto the street for a walk. As we approached the corner of Seventh Avenue, I noticed (and heard) two enormous dogs barking ferociously. They looked angry, maybe even crazy, but at least they were tied to the newsstand. I edged away from them.

"Go ahead!" said the guy by the newsstand. He sounded so confident. "Go right up to them! They know who you are."

"They do?"

"Yes," he said, warmly. Apparently the dogs were only pretending they were ferociously poised to attack bystanders. They were just putting on a show, the guy said. I decided to trust the newsman and hoped the dogs and I would like each other. I assumed that Nada felt the same way, and I thought he was right behind me. Thinking that he was, I was inspired to go right up to the dogs. I did, and they got all quiet and amicable. I offered a few sincere, friendly pats on each of their heads, studying at close range their moist and tremendously sharp fangs. Before walking away, I looked behind me—Nada and Parvati had disappeared! And the moment I walked away the dogs resumed barking like hounds from hell. It was a strange way to show they wanted to be patted.

10

A Stroll
around Herald Square

IT WAS A WONDER TO WALK WITH NADA on a street in New York
City. So, when the lesson ended that day, I again joined the odd couple
on a trek to Clark Willoughby's on Thirty Seventh Street. They needed
to pick up some photographs. I noticed something about Nada: the look
of childlike wonder—it was all a marvelous dream on tape unrolling
before him, the sights and sounds, nothing at all like the Himalayas.
The master of vibrations was having a good time.

It was raining, and Parvati had warned Nada to prepare for rain.
He said he'd pray to end the rain, and chuckled as he stepped out on to
the street—dressed for the wildest rainstorm. And yet, the moment we
stepped out, the rain stopped and the sun came out.

"See," he said, "God take care of rain."

I wondered if he really believed that he was instrumental in causing the rain to stop. Or was it just a coincidence? In any event, he came
out prepared—he had God to rely on *and* he brought his umbrella and
raincoat.

At first I walked uneasily with him, thinking he might find cross-
ing Herald Square at rush hour more taxing than reaching the shore

of enlightenment. But he was perfectly at ease with the madness of traffic and the chaotic bustle of Manhattan humanity. I had forgotten how keen his eyesight was, how alert to everything alive and particular around him. He strode right out into the traffic, trailing his orange sari, with holy indifference to rules of red and green light. When he got into a fix with a car coming, he did as other New Yorkers do and ran for his life, which the roundish monk did with admirable agility.

He knew exactly the location of Clark Willoughby and emphasized that there were two entrances to the camera shop. Inside, he showed me around and remarked on the advanced technology of the art of photography. The slides we picked up were immediately subjected to careful scrutiny. They were mostly of Nada, taken by Parvati, with towering buildings and swirls of motley humanity in the background.

After picking up the slides, we began to saunter back. Nada seemed content and well-disposed toward the great spectacle of Maya, the hectic denizens of space and time all around him, coming and going. Suddenly, he stopped and peered at something across the street.

It was a huge bicentennial window display of David Hamburger's, consisting of all the presidents of the United States, with Gerald Ford right in the middle, his face painted much brighter than the others. The display captured Nada's attention, so we crossed the street. The first thing Nada noticed was what a poor replica the little dummy of ford was. Curious about what was inside, we ventured into David Hamburger's, which was normally closed to the public since they only sold wholesale.

I announced to two gentlemen standing together looking imperiously idle that Swamiji was a wandering minstrel from India, an ambassador of good will, and asked if they would permit us to browse the contents of their store. The two men were instantly receptive, the graceful form of Parvati adding to the charm, and one of them solemnly guided us around the displays: some were of spring and autumn and some of holidays like Christmas and Thanksgiving Day. Emerald paper trees rustled from mechanical breezes and winsome-faced elves sawed wood for weary farmers. It was a fairy land of iconic consumerism, a shiny mythology of the commercial and the advertisable.

Nada took in the extravagant showcasing with pleasure. "Wonderful," he kept saying, and thanked the man who showed us around. It was all a dream for Nada, a strange parade of phenomena, a movie produced in the mind of God. Some scientists, after a few days of tests, discovered that Nada apparently did not dream. It occurred to me that perhaps he didn't dream while he was asleep because while he was awake, he experienced the world as if it were a dream. Perhaps if we got into the habit of seeing all of waking life as if it were a dream, we might stop dreaming and need much less sleep. Perhaps the more "real" we take the world to be in our waking hours, the more stressful and greater our need to refresh ourselves in dream reality.

Our stroll together ended, and on my way home I recalled a brief exchange we had after the lesson officially ended—a paradox. I had to make friends with death before I could understand the mysteries of music, Nada said. I was not quite sure what he meant. How do we learn to dance to the tune and the rhythm of Yama, the god of death?

This was not an easy assignment, especially coming out of a music lesson. Philosophy was the practice of death, Plato explained in the *Phaedo*; a way to detach oneself from one's body, and begin to tune into forms of consciousness not weighed down by the body. Philosophy, as suggested by Plato's thought, is about altering our consciousness, by weaning ourselves from attachment to our mundane mental life. Music, as we'll see, converges with Plato's seemingly strange idea of philosophy.

11

Krishna's Garden

ALIDA HAD A CLASS BEFORE MINE but failed to show up. Swami Nada was perplexed; she was usually on time.

"I wait and wait but Alida never come," he said, in a tone of genuine concern.

It occurred to me she may well have been off again on another tour into what was beginning to appear like a dangerous flight from reality, and I was distracted by her behavior, but the master viber pushed the tabla before me.

"Little tabla," he said. It was foolish to resist, so I began, murmuring, as I struck the drums, "*daghi, natin, naka, dhina.*"

"Yes," he said with approval. He beat out the pattern—and the slow steady rhythm instantly calmed me.

I was to strike the very same spot on the drum each time. I resisted being so precise, beating the drum on the same spot, but I was intrigued by the idea of fusing the precision of mathematics with the magic of music.

"Think about what you doing—timing," Nada said.

I had forgotten what I was doing—I became more mechanical when my attention lapsed. My left hand had always to perform something different from the right. When the right hand held, the left was supposed to come up. But unless I paid attention, the right hand would come up when the left hand did, or the right hand would stay when the left stayed.

It was easy to see the mechanical side of my nature writ large, and at the same time the curious ability of the intentional mind, with which, with slow and patient effort, I could learn to command the diverse elements of my bodily self to perform their allotted roles while remaining in harmony with each other. The right hemisphere of my brain controlled the left side of my body and the left hemisphere the right side—but what controlled and harmonized the two brain hemispheres? The frontal lobes, I presumed. Or rather, *myself*, by means of my frontal lobes. I am not my frontal lobes—but I do like to remain on good terms with them.

It was part of Nada's method *to never suggest a self-defeating thought*. Wherever I missed the mark, he stopped and went back to something simpler, something I could execute correctly. This made it easier to approach the more difficult obstacle, and helped me muster my confidence.

"Yes," he said, after I started to get it right, "understanding first." He launched into a brilliant caper on the tabla, displaying his mastery with gusto. He repeated the refrain that understanding was primary, and that the rest would come automatically. Mind was master, and mind was not a specialized talent. By mind he meant more than concepts and inference, but a way of focusing attention, a self-fashioning conscious power.

"First, *sa, ri, ga, ma,* how much difficulty, now coming easy," he said, laughing, recalling to me the hard time I had taking the first steps in counting. It was like looking back on a previous incarnation. If I moved to a new plateau, he'd remind me of the distance traversed, invite me to remember my older, struggling self.

I began to drum, with fewer mistakes, each hand striking out its own rhythm but both in unison. I was starting to come together with myself. It was a gratifying sensation that felt like soft waves of energy flowing through me.

He stopped, suddenly, and reached for some photographs. "A photographer came here. He wants picture exhibition, tonight he's coming." The photographs were interesting and Nada displayed each one slowly and carefully. Many were of his hands moving gracefully over the swarmandala.

"He say nothing—here, there—tek, tek, tek . . ." and he made a gesture imitating the photographer moving about him rapidly clicking his camera.

"So what are your latest plans, Swamiji—where are you going?" I asked him, as I looked at the photographs.

"Everything coming correct," he said. I noted how Nada's favorite metaphor took in every aspect of life. His life was music. "For Swamiji, anything he like," he said, referring to Vishnu. "I told you, I wait. I want going lovely. Bad, going out sudden. Fighting then." I never quite understood why Nada and Parvati were under some kind of pressure to leave the ashram. The politics of enlightenment was apparently not as smooth or gracious as one might imagine.

He smiled at me and said, "Your mind, something heavy—I show photographs." He had deliberately distracted me. We went on till I got what I was supposed to get right. Just at the moment that I did, he looked at me and we burst into laughter.

"*Raga arabi,*" he said, as we turned to the new song I was learning. I handed him the tabla and he pushed the harmonium toward me.

"*Vranda wanaka krishanykanya,*" we sang over and over again. He drummed along, correcting me on the intonation or rhythm or fingering whenever I made the slightest mistake. Then I noticed a shift. With every repetition of the word *vranda*, meaning "garden," I felt a deep resonance in my chest. With exhilarating effect, I began to receive images of the supremely seductive Krishna, who takes away our worldly mind and makes the tiger and the cow lie down together in amity.

"*Sabaki ankhoanka tara*—write," he said, and sang the new phrase of the song, syllable by syllable, giving the corresponding notes *ma, pa, pa, ma,* and so on. First he taught me to sing the phrase, then the fingering on the harmonium.

At this point I had little idea what the song was really about but I was happy to let the mantric magic work whatever it could upon me. The image of the flute-blowing Lord Krishna shining like a star in his garden played well. Indeed, music, as I was learning, was one way back to my internal Garden of Eden. The enchanter Krishna, so charmingly compatible with our senses and even our imperfect feelings, sends out his amorous flute call to the world, gently beckoning us to return to the music of paradise. Nothing apocalyptic, no special force, very "smooth," to use one of Nada's favorite words. A happy divinity luring us away from the torturous discords of being struggling humans. How superior to those pious bullies of the world who try to moralize us into rectitude.

The lesson came to an end. I said good afternoon to Nada, and stepped out into the noise and murky air of Seventh Avenue. Meandering through crowds and traffic, from time to time forgetting where I was, I intoned *vranda wanaka in tal keherawa,* an excellent walking rhythm.

I liked this celestial song; it was a thread to follow on walks that might lead me to the pleasures of Krishna's garden.

12

Silence at the Center
of the Drum

AS WE ARRANGED THE INSTRUMENTS today to begin the lesson some words passed between us concerning the problem Nada was facing. He wanted now to leave in a way that was "lovely"—bringing new life into an old, worn word.

"I don't want fighting—I want love," he said in measured tones. He wanted to leave in friendship with Vishnu.

"After he agree—and I give him money—whatever he want—then I go."

Nada decided to comply with whatever wishes and conditions Vishnu set down. There was an issue of money between these hardscrabble mystics. The amount was probably piddling, but not for Nada and Parvati.

"Your power is in your music," I said, and added, "anyway, he's not that powerful—he's only a man."

"Yes," he replied, "but *rules* . . ." he went on, raising his voice a little, and then laughed and hummed a few notes.

There were restrictive laws that the power of his music could not change. These laws were a constant source of "risk"—Nada could not, strictly speaking, teach and make his music unless it was under the sponsorship of a religious organization. Vishnu, in a real and worldly sense, had power over the ghandarva and his consort.

"Police come!" he smiled again. Nada definitely loved his freedom.

"I like bird in cage," he complained.

"You could sing your way out of any cage," I said, smiling back. Nada in jail? The unthinkable can and quite often does happen. It's a plain fact of history that often the best of humans are attacked, jailed, hanged, decapitated, gassed, clubbed, poisoned, crucified, burned at the stake, or otherwise made to disappear. At that moment I thought of my friend, Alida, a gifted healer-therapist who introduced me to Nada. I had recently learned that she was arrested for loud and unreasonable behavior. She was calling people up at three o'clock in the morning and ranting about the chief resident of the White House. Alida—my trust-worthy healer friend—incarcerated in a madhouse!

The rules of the real world are not the rules of divine music. The same man can be master in one world and a bird in a cage in another. Suddenly he tossed the violet coverings off his drums and began to beat on them. He was determined to advance my drumming skills. He insisted it would be easy because I knew all the essentials. I was in fact drawn to drumming, a way to tune into the rhythms of the heart; and also, a way for the two halves of my brain to practice coming together.

"Don't worry," he kept saying. He told me to beat on a pot or a table top, or even hum the rhythms in my mind, and not to be too literal about real drums. If anything, my experience with Nada was a long lesson about the spiritual dangers of being too literal-minded.

He illustrated his point by drumming more and more softly until he finished by performing gestures in perfect silence. The sounds he was making had retreated to the etheric plane, into the *anahata,* the "unstruck" world of sound. More than once he drummed on my arm, or on my head, or on the floor—anywhere it was possible to start the beat and slip into the flow.

The drum was not the point but a certain mental stance that could express itself in any medium—sound, color, touch, breath, whatever. Nada suddenly broke into a garland of chants all in tala dadara. He wanted to show me how easy it was. Once I knew the fingering and counting, drumming would be mine to conjure with. I'd have the key to many songs. Each song, however, had to be learned anew—new raga, new notes—whereas the rhythmic pattern was a universal power that brought all songs and, in principle, all forms and styles of consciousness together.

"Count *dadara*," he said. As I counted, he drummed in unison, and I felt a live current of warm energy. He drummed and sang while I counted—once I made a mistake and clapped on *tona*.

"Tona empty," he said. Emptiness was essential to the flow—the power of doing nothing, of letting things be. In a sense it was really quite easy. I had to learn how to quit making useless efforts, and I had to work on timing and on avoiding unnecessary force.

"No force, not anything special, very smoothly," he kept saying as he showed me the fingering for the tala. The Indian tabla are a pair of drums; one is larger than the other, each with a different sound, though the face of both drums is similar. Near the center is a circular, dark area of material which, curiously, mutes the sound. Silence is at the center of the drum. The center of the drum is a borderland between the heard and the unheard, the visible and the invisible.

I recalled an idea from that strange art form called parapsychology—the notion of "release of effort" that is associated with paranormality, and the idea that "trying too hard" to achieve an effect often turns out to be counter-productive. I did my best to stay in an easy attitude, listening for the unstruck sound in my mind, feeling the pulse coming steady. All of it was oriented toward the great enigma of coming correct with my Self.

Nada liked to show how I could practice without any instrument. He pretended he was riding a bus, closed his eyes, and began tapping on his thighs, very casually.

"See, you sit, no work, very easy," he remarked.

"This is true," I said, "providing you practice relentlessly." He shrugged my remark off and told me not to worry. Nada would teach music to any human being who sat beside him that wanted to learn. There was no mystique of passing on his knowledge to an elect few. It didn't matter who you were; you received the same patience and good will. Never testy or begrudging, Nada was always at one with himself.

"*Jaya Sita Ram,*" he sang.

"What does 'Sita Ram' mean?" I asked.

"Sita is wife of the Lord, of Ram. Parvati is wife of Vishnu . . ."

"Many gods!" I exclaimed.

"Thirty-three million," he replied. "But all are one," he was quick to add. He touched my hair, and said: "Many hairs, one head." That, I thought, was the most concise statement of the philosophy of religion I had ever heard. The names of Sita, Parvati, and Rhada echoed in my mind and I was pleased to note that each divinity had a suitable consort.

"God is one," he continued, "only names differ. You say *water,* in Sanskrit *neer,* in Hindi *pani.*"

He paused for a moment; he was traveling in his mind.

"In India no one says 'good morning'—they say 'Sita Ram' and take God's name."

I casually mentioned that I would like to go with him to India one day. He seemed unaverse to the idea and pointed out that we would be able to travel first class cheap! We went back to chanting Java Guru Deva, going through all the names of the devas and powers, forcing them into the mold of the four beats that would fit them into the chant. He wove all the gods together into a single song, which he emphatically wanted me to appreciate. As he sang, I remembered the day I discovered the Vedanta Society in New York City. Inside, I read on the wall in large, ornate print words from the Rig Veda: "Truth is one; men call it variously."

That hit me full square, the liberating idea of one transcendent reality that people experience and name in their own culture-bound way. I never forgot those words that seemed, then and now, correct. I was grateful to Nada for refreshing my memory of that all-harmonizing piece of philosophical truth.

Just as I had my association of the Rig Veda, Nada sang of Swamiji and Michaelji! As if to underline my intuition, it seemed that *any* name became a name of power if properly intoned, according to numbers, and fitted into the cosmic formulas.

He commented on the *ji,* which he attached to my name to fill out the requisite four beats and which was an indication of topmost respect.

"In India first, middle, down," he observed, referring to the Indian social hierarchy.

"Here king, president, servant, you say, 'How are you?'—all are same."

"Yes," I said, "it's what we call democracy. We have our own little Rig Veda, also known as The Declaration of Independence."

Nada peered back at me, but said nothing. At the end of the lesson I mentioned I was going to have dinner with Alida, that she was released from the hospital and was available for a meeting. Nada said he'd come along for a brief visit and called for Parvati.

13

Nada Visits a Disturbed Student

IN A SHORT WHILE WE FOUND OURSELVES around Alida's great wooden table in her loft on West 16th Street. We sat in a circle and drank coffee.

"Everyday I pray for Alida," Nada said, smiling and patting her on the back very warmly.

I looked around the loft. The musical instruments were piled in a compact heap; books, paintings, photographs were all neatly in place. Alida was busy trying to bring back some order into her life. She had been on a strange journey and needed to piece her home back together again.

"I was really with God all the time," she said, "but nobody would let me alone to enjoy her."

Nada smiled as she spoke. It was not clear how much of it he allowed to fully penetrate his consciousness.

"I got very angry when nobody would share my God consciousness—I tried to kick a judge in the shins." I had not heard of this, and wasn't sure if she was being sardonic—or if she kicked, or tried to kick, a real judge.

"I wasn't sure if this got to him," she added. Alida then offered an explanation of her recent episodes of madness, her behaviors that brought the police to her. She seemed taken with certain parallels between what she deemed her god-intoxicated psychosis and Nada's customary serenely centered state.

"I got swept away in a tidal wave of kundalini energy—I didn't know how to control it—and that's why I needed you."

There wasn't enough milk in his coffee, so Nada asked Parvati to fetch him some; meanwhile he played with his black cane and drummed on the wooden table.

"It was when I went mad that I hardly slept and stopped dreaming— like you, Swamiji," Alida said, pleased with the comparison.

"But I never get angry," Nada said, pointing to the limits of the comparison.

"Well, you see," Alida replied, "in the Pentecostal Play they cast me as Yahweh—an angry god."

This was true. Alida had been rehearsing for an off-off-Broadway production of a Pentecostal Play in which she was cast as Yahweh. Unfortunately, she failed to arrive for her performance on opening night, though she apparently enjoyed a period of stardom in the wards of Bellevue.

I thought about the difference between Alida and Nada not dreaming. Alida's dreams spilled over into waking day, where she acted out her desires and became an angry god who kicked the judges of this world and bought a hundred dollars' worth of stout for a banquet of self-healing. With the monk-musician, all his dreams are acted out in songs, and the wrath of Yahweh he beats out of himself on his tabla.

We chatted amiably a while longer until it was time for the two musicians to return to the ashram. Alida and I rambled downtown toward an Indian restaurant on Carmine Street. She was savoring every sight and sound of the city.

"What do you think triggered the kundalini that blew you away?" I asked.

She went through a number of possibilities. "Maybe it was Al's machismo conga drums, his rampant belching of lust and rage that tipped me off."

Al was a person who used Alida's loft on Friday nights as a theater of free expression. For a while it served as a place to meet once a week for a session of group chant, primal scream, and poetic howling. I sometimes wondered if all the wild vibes unleashed at those Friday night blasts lingered on somehow in Alida's living space and affected her mental life.

"Or maybe it was Nada that really did it," she said. "No one ever really totally accepted me as he did."

"I don't get it—what did he do?" Powerful emanations from Nada apparently could stir up strange impulses.

"Nothing, nothing at all," she replied, "he didn't *do* anything, he just let me be, I could feel him let me be. With every human being I've ever known, I sensed some limit, some restraint, like 'not too far.' With Swamiji there was none. I guess I sort of lost my bearings, something inside me suddenly felt insanely free . . ."

"Did it scare you?"

"No, it thrilled me! Nada wanted me to go with him to the big yoga convention in Chicago—and drum with him there before a huge audience. It was strange to be suddenly trusted like that. My defenses had nothing to work against. Some weird power in me began to bubble up. His silence released me."

"The silence at the center of the drum," I muttered, thinking back to my lesson.

"What do you mean?" she said.

"Nothing—only it's plain now why love is so rare."

"Too much would drive us all crazy—there wouldn't be enough Bellevues to take in all the world's truly inspired lovers," she said ruefully.

"Don't worry, it's not happening."

"Not if you rely on people like the guard at North Five," she said, a disturbed look coming across her face. I assumed this was some person who gave her a hard time, but I ignored her remark.

I looked up and down Sixth Avenue. Cars were honking, noisome fumes casting a lurid hue on the horizon. Down and out time for New York City. My eye wandered above the traffic and followed the patches of sunlight on the building faces.

"You have to admit that Nada is a menace to society," Alida said, a glint of mischief in her clear blue eyes.

"Should we inform the people at the Immigration Office?" I asked.

"Not necessary, they'll get him if they want to. They'll put him and Parvati in jail for being unworldly."

"We're joking—aren't we?"

"What about Jesus?"

"Jesus lacked one thing that Nada has," I replied.

"The swarmandala," she said.

14

The Jungle
as Music Critic

I SAT DOWN WHILE HARI, a fellow student, was finishing his lesson. I rarely bumped into Hari. I noticed he seemed distressed that he was making so many mistakes; I could well sympathize with him. Nada was prodding him out of his low spirits, encouraging him to focus his attention, but then Nada's thoughts wandered back to his homeland in the Himalayas. I got the feeling he was musing on scenes of his life that he was missing.

"When I singing, sitting silent," he intoned, referring to the animals that sat with him as he played in the ashram in Rishikesh. Then his face lit up, as if he were about to tell us something wonderful. Nada was a born actor; he always used his voice to act out a thought, his gestures to dramatize the main point. His arguments were movements of his body, his face the visible voice of his music.

He was telling Hari that his silence only meant that he was playing all right. It was when you made a mistake that he spoke or made a sign. So likewise in the Himalayas where he used to play and sing, when he was performing, the animals that dwelled with him kept a judicious silence.

"Tiger watching me by door—little mistake," he said, and imitated the look of an affronted tiger. The image of the animals of the jungle silently observing his practice, and reminding him whenever he made a mistake, struck Hari and me as hilarious. Nada knew he had our attention, so he continued.

"Cobra also very unhappy—playing well, cobra very nice, very lovely." He looked at me—"little wrong," and he made a comical gesture indicating the way a cobra might start up with disapproval.

"They'd really go wild if I played there," I said.

Apparently his music was so excellent that the wild animals became tame enough to be fed from human hands; the stories about Orpheus and Francis of Assisi may not have been just mythical.

"There are many photos of tigers and snakes, cobras and monkeys getting milk every day—that was when there was no electric light, no people, no buildings. The very friendly tigers all gone now since people came. Parvati has seen all this. Monkeys never sitting still—music play—sitting silent with their eyes closed."

He mimicked the look of a monkey attentively listening with eyes closed.

"So music can quiet the mad monkey of the mind," I said.

He laughed, adding: "A child cries, and if there is some nice singing, child becomes silent. Music is the secret to peace of mind. Animals like music, you see, snakes especially." He quoted something from the Vedas: "*Sesurvati pasurvati veni penevesant* (All things want to change into music)."

"You weren't afraid they'd bite you, Swamiji?" Hari asked.

"No, never," he replied.

Hari was wondering what happened to the snakes and other wild creatures when Nada quit charming them with his music: "And when you stop singing, they just go away?"

"Oh, no," he said in a tone of great earnestness, "first day I start singing, very big cobra there sitting—door then I open." He spoke slowly, intoning thoughtfully, and clapped once: "I close door. Long time I at window saw him there sitting. He was very lovely, and after twenty minutes, half an hour, all calm, all calm."

It seemed that the cobra enjoyed the concert so much that he made it a practice to return for many repeat performances. "And after again snake returns and enjoys, and now I open door. Oh, yes, very friendly snake. And then I give milk." He paused, and said, "I have photo."

Music is Nada's way of making friends with everything alive in nature. But would it work with the landlords of ordinary civilized life?

Then he told of a tiger and a doubting lady:

"One day a lady heard that Swamiji at three o'clock in morning makes music. Never, she said, this is bogus. And people told her, you can go and see him. And so she came, but a tiger sitting by the door was listening to my music. Tiger night-time, eyes are very powerful, man not see but tiger see everything."

So we have an image of the tiger watching Nada's door in the dark from a short distance, and coming upon this scene of enchantment is a curious Western lady who thinks it's all bogus.

"She come and knocks on door. I surprised." He makes a knocking gesture. "I don't see anything." Meanwhile, his all-seeing admirer and ally, the tiger, was silently observing the early-morning caller. She knocked a second time. Nada noticed the lady and the tiger in the midst of his profound meditation. Assuming a serious countenance, he said, referring to the lady blithely unaware of her peril: "I take her inside."

And once she was safe and in: "What is it? You not see tiger there?" No doubt the inquisitive lady got more than she bargained for—not just Swami Nada but also a music-loving tiger!

Anyway, it was lovely there before the men came with their electric lights, and their nervous revolvers. Gone are the lovely monkeys and snakes and dogs and cows of the old ashram.

"Chidananda, with cats and dogs and monkeys, altogether, eating from one big plate; Vishnu also always playing with monkeys, very friendly there."

During the lesson we drifted into drumming. I kept striking the drum with more force than was necessary. Was this a parable of the human condition or just my problem? On *da* the right index finger holds, on *ghi* it snaps. It was a rhythm of holding and letting go, and there could be no accident or confusion as to when to hold and when to let go. That, I suppose, can be generalized to the game of life: when to let go and when not to let go.

After practicing a while the fingering for each separate hand, we began very slowly to synchronize the action of both hands. As usual, that part was not easy—simultaneously to hold and let go, the right hand holding, the left hand coming up, opposing tendencies balanced. My right hand wanted to come up with my left, or my left stay down with my right, and each mechanically followed the other. I had to think about what I was doing constantly. I had to de-automatize the automatic and seize my breath of inspiration. Every time I missed, slipped, drifted, Swami Nada would stop the game and slow me almost to a halt.

"Very smoothly," he incanted, "and all together coming."

We then went on to chanting, reviewing the ragas I had learned, and I suddenly found myself playing and singing without worry. I got into the swing of it and it seemed that my inner saboteur had gone fishing, allowing me to sing on with Nada. I looked up at him and was amazed to see that as he was drumming away, he had tipped over to a curious angle *and he was sleeping very soundly!* I was apparently not making any mistakes, so he took a little nap—even while his fingers drummed out rhythms in tune with me. I was unable to prevent myself from laughing out loud, and suddenly he started up and beat on the drum with renewed enthusiasm, playfully trying to distract me from my focus.

15

The Secret of Never Getting Tired

GIOVANNI, MY FLUTE TEACHER, came along and sat with me during the lesson. We were out of the city and visiting an ashram in Upstate New York. Young instructor of the West sat before old master of the East. The two musicians greeted each other amicably. Giovanni of the West looked tired; he was frazzled from being on the road. Nada of the East had been on the road with two hours of dreamless sleep a night. The twenty-one-year-old jazz man was a prodigious dreamer. Desire and frustration buffeted him at every step of the way. He called it paying his dues.

"How are you, Giovanni?" Nada asked.

"Tired," he replied.

"Tired? What is tired?" Nada said with unabashed delight. He proceeded to describe the labors of his lifestyle, and to catalogue his various virtues, stating that ordinary human fatigue was a thing unknown to him. And it was true. Nada always left his followers stumbling and panting behind him. There was, for example, the drummer of Bombay who took him on in a musical contest. The poor man ended up in the hospital for *four months* nursing his limp, swollen arms.

"What's the secret of never getting tired?" I asked.

"Anything I doing, what doing, I never think," he replied immediately, "everything He doing."

In my own way I understood this to be a description of a man completely integrated with his subliminal mind or self; somehow he has contrived to unite his conscious ego with his subliminal motor and perceptual apparatus. His conscious life was in tune with his more powerful subconscious Self, and as a result he suffered from few if any sensations of tiresome effort.

"So that's why you don't get tired; you're not worrying about anything. You leave everything up to Him."

"*He* does it. I never think anything," he said with strong emphasis. There was a quality in his voice that silenced all discursive scruples.

"We are riding in car," he said, making a vivid gesture that put me on a highway across Montana, "we are sitting inside, sleeping and watching hill and city passing, going and passing—but driver always looking, always awake, always careful. *He* take care." His voice rose with excitement.

"So, God is your chauffeur, and that's why you never get tired?"

"Yah," he said, with a tone of, *of course*.

"No petrol I think, no maps I need, no directions I worry, I don't care red light, green light. I resting. He driving."

Let go, let God was a New Age maxim. It was old hat for Nada.

I pumped him for more information on the secret of never getting tired. What I got comes to this. First, a long life dedicated to a sattvic (light and clear) diet. Indeed, all experience is food. Eat lightly, and regard all experience lightly. The more weight we attach to our experiences, the more we load them with ponderous significance, the more fatigued we become. But learn and practice the names of power, Om and Klim and Rama and Hari and Sita, ad infinitum. But why work the body so hard? There are many who wear themselves out just sitting still!

"No marriage," he said with contained emphasis. He joked about the hassle of having property, how it bogs you down and makes you think, and how he owned everything by owning nothing.

Last, maybe the main point, is that Nada never worried. To worry is to tire yourself, to consume the precious energy of spirit. Why do we worry? This may be the original sin—we forget the gap between what we think and what there is. So do what must be done, and don't worry. It's all on film, and we might as well enjoy the show. We're just passengers in the car of destiny, and God is driving—so the ultimate quintessential wisdom of all time is really quite simple. It occurred to me that Nada's message was similar to the message of an eighteenth-century spiritual classic by Jean-Pierre de Caussade, *Abandonment to Divine Providence*. Caussade describes how we should interpret whatever happens to us in life as an opportunity to abandon ourselves to the divine will and mind. Whatever happens, no matter how bad it may appear at that moment—regard it as a necessary part of your journey.

He went on, "I tell you, we take nothing when die—so what is worth trouble? I left ashram in New York—never think now. Finish. *My* property! I thinking always—take care, this, that, worry. Whole world my property, own nothing, care about nothing."

"And everywhere your students follow you around," I said.

"I never alone sitting," he agreed, always eager to share the divine satisfaction of his existence.

"And I never thinking," he said, returning to the keystone of his extremely practical but daunting metaphysics, which, I was beginning to see, boiled down to two words in the imperative mood: *Stop thinking!*

I admired the sheer economy of Nada's style of existence. His mind, that frequent instrument of self-immolation, was used sparingly and never to his own disadvantage. I get the point about the futility of so much wasted mental energy on fruitless effort and futile speculation. It is fine to laud the virtues of not thinking, I thought to myself. However, there are times in the real world, when to not think—to not reflect, protest, or speak out—is just plain wrong.

"But Swamiji," I said, "this is not so easy for me. My dharma is thinking, thinking about thinking and thinking about not thinking."

He smiled and said, "My dharma is music. I sitting there singing, I don't know anything." He repeated: "I don't know anything." He said it in a way that seemed so humble and earnest, I had to restrain myself from hugging him.

I thought of the numberless times I lacerated myself with my own thoughts. Truly, I believe we underestimate to what degree we are our own enemies. But to fully realize this, and make it work for us, we need to become skilled self-observers. This can be very difficult because we are so concerned with how others perceive us.

"Not anywhere in world eighty-one-year-old men like me," Nada then added, perhaps exaggerating a little. But then he qualified his remark: "Nowhere, unless you have mind control."

He pushed the tabla before me and said I should "show" him tala keherawa. I hesitated. The truth is I wanted to learn more about Nada Brahmananda.

Still, he got me to pace myself, and I was able to sustain an unbroken thread of drumming as Nada pranced about on the harmonium, jostling me with odd rhythms, sudden rushes of energy. I knew my part in the game was not to be distracted or thrown off balance. I was to keep to the rhythm I had chosen, even if I hear bombs exploding around me. His rhythms strained against my simple, constant flow, but together the life and harmony of the song was saved. The jostles slurred into my pulse, the discordant notes became servants of the final coming together. We were making melodies of consciousness, filling the air around us with vibrations formed from our minds. At that moment, it flashed on me that Socrates was wrong. Music is the greatest philosophy.

After the lesson, Giovanni and I took a walk with Nada. It was a long walk, up and down several hills in upstate New York, until we reached a main highway and stopped. Nada liked to walk right on the yellow lines between two lanes. There weren't many cars on Orange

Turnpike but sometimes they came up suddenly on a hill and Nada would dart to safety. His casual way of stopping on the middle of the turnpike, leaning back on his cane and surveying a passing buzzard or rock of unusual shape, made me nervous. I found myself praying to the devas to keep an eye on Nada. "Suppose two cars on both sides of the road came at the same time toward you—which way would you run?" I asked, hoping I could scare him to one side of the road.

"Never happen," he observed with brash confidence.

Suddenly a car came roaring over the hill at well over sixty miles an hour. Nada froze for an instant and looked at me. I grabbed him by the arm and yanked him away from the oncoming vehicle.

"Woman driving," he commented dryly, as he stepped back to the middle of the road, pointing with his cane at some spots of orange paint between the two yellow lines.

"This car man driving," he said, having heard the motor, quiet and slower-sounding, of an approaching car.

The car passed, driven by a woman. Nada said nothing. I said, "Swamiji, ladies can drive very correct!" We walked in silence for a while, Nada at a steady clip, twirling and tapping his cane rhythmically, as he peered about with his eyes that could see twenty-five miles. With an utter lightness of spirit he hiked on along that winding highway. His merry gait spoke of indifference to anything on the other side of the hill.

"Do you think he might give me something to practice while I'm on the road?" Giovanni said to me in a whisper.

"Ask him."

Nada paused to admire the garden bordering a beautifully well-kept Catholic church we were passing.

"Many humble trees," he remarked with admiration. He called willow trees humble because of the downward bend of their branches. Several sisters with pale faces strolled by and smiled faintly at the Indian monk.

"Very clean," he said with approval. The roads of India were strewn with garbage and debris, he had mentioned several times. He noticed differences, but never judged. Judgments are efforts—very tiring.

Nada suddenly stopped on Orange Turnpike, surrounded by mountains wrapped in clear sunlight, and said: "I never think we be here like this." He seemed grateful and astonished at just being where he was.

"This is all on film—reel unrolling," and he glanced upward, alluding to the Eternal Director.

"Like a movie set," he said, "all arrange—not real." He raised his arm, cupped his hand, and made a sweeping gesture that captured perfectly the image of King Kong flailing at airplanes from the top of the Empire State Building. He had seen a recent remake of the original film. According to Nada, life may be likened to a Hollywood spectacular, entertaining no doubt but at best the stuff of dreams.

We walked on in silence. I thought to myself: *Not* to see the world as real; that might serve as an effective stress-reducer. Is it part of the secret of never getting tired? Is this the solution to all the stress inescapably woven into the fabric of life? Thinking it's all so real and weighty is the problem—was that the way out, to live life as if it were a dream, a movie?

Again Nada stopped and looked around: "Watch film!" and he waved his arm around, taking in the panorama of the twilit horizon. The sun was sinking behind the humble willow trees and the air was cooling. Nada's declaration that what was happening at that moment was a film unrolling from the Reel of Eternity came to life. I reflected on the phantasmal reality of everything around me, and felt a softening of the boundaries of my body. In my mind, I wandered out of body into open space and saw down below three men walking on Orange Turnpike.

"Nothing to do—just watch the film," I said, slipping back into my normal focus.

Nada made a sound as of water rushing down a waterfall, which he meant to evoke as the running reel of time. He further explained that on this cosmic movie set of Maya we own nothing, and that even our bodies are "rent-bodies." The obsession with ownership is fatiguing, he was fond of reminding us. Then he said one word and paused, "Help," he said. He pointed toward a bush near the road that was humming with bees. "All nature help man—but man not help man."

After the long walk we returned to the ashram. It was almost dark. Nada said how much he enjoyed the outing, gave us his blessings and retired to his room. That night, at about ten in the evening, Giovanni and I wandered down on the slope of the hill beside the Main House where Nada was in his room. The moon's reflection glittered on the dark lake. Softly we played raga malakauns on our flutes, hoping that Nada in the Main House might hear some echoes of the songs he taught us.

16

Last Group Lesson with the Ghandarva

NADA GAVE A GROUP LESSON TODAY. A lesson in music but also a few hints on the art of living. We sat in a group around him. He beckoned us to sit closer. It was no use retreating to an inconspicuous corner in this very odd classroom. Nada was aware of every person in his presence. He respected neither your rank in the world nor your defensive attitudes. It was clear what you had to do. Take hold of yourself, become aware of your mind, and concentrate on the task and moment at hand. For that we need Nada's ever-elusive "full mind."

The quality of our effort was transparent to Nada's penetrating gaze. Few were willing to merely loiter in his presence, so our numbers thinned to a small group.

"My name, Nada Brahmananda—*Nada* mean 'divine sound.' *Brahmananda* mean 'happiness.'" That's how he introduced himself—as the embodiment of the happiness that sacred music can create. How wonderfully outrageous to go through life bearing such a name!

He beamed at us, a smile playing around his lips, but we were determined to look on with grave concentration.

"In India they have word for house not singing God's name—cemetery."

Nada was here to teach us how to escape the cemetery of ordinary mindless existence.

"Wherever singing, heaven," he added at last, with a sweet touch.

Having made these introductory remarks, he started to teach the group to count. As you know by now, for Nada his brand of counting was the key to unlocking the mystery of being. First was tala, which he drilled into me, the omnipresent rhythmic pattern, the four beats that you hear everywhere: in the wind, in the hum of a motor, in a concerto of Bach, in the sighs of lovers. To count *dhagi natin naka dhina* was to walk all the roads of life, to burrow into the secret heart of all things that move. He added the curious observation that this tala was best for *brahmacharya,* chastity—an alien concept, for the most part, to most of us selfish gene machines sitting there.

Once you learn to count, you have the key to the chanting power of the divine names, the great arsenal of archetypes and their healing vibrations. But without counting correctly, there is no rhythm, no flow, no music, no bliss, and no liberation from death and rebirth. Moreover, counting correctly was key to when Siva and Shakti dance together.

"Music without tala, without balance, like writing with pen on lake. You do? You write letter to friend on water?"

An older man was sitting on a squeaky chair. Nada stopped and invited him to take to the floor, but the man chose to seek a quieter chair. Chairs were changed and Nada resumed counting.

"What you do?" He whirled around and pointed at the older man when he clapped out of tune with the group. To make matters worse, his new chair was still annoyingly squeaky.

"You come here," Nada commanded the squeaky man whose name was Roland, and who spoke with a polite drawl which seemed always to be begging pardon for something.

"Oh, thank you very much," Roland said. The old monk took the man's hand and tried to direct it in the correct clapping motion.

"Stiff! Why stiff?" Nada cried out, making a funny face imitating excessive strain. "No force—loose." He dangled his hands limply and tried to communicate the correct attitude. The man was smiling, and eager to learn, but also looked stiff and uncomfortable.

Nada fared better with young women, pliable and more receptive. The men all clap too quickly and use too much force, but one young woman was having difficulties. She was not bringing her hand up to her ear after she clapped and she was indiscriminately using her index finger, which Nada was fond of denouncing as the "ego finger," the finger that points accusingly and makes too many demands.

The woman sported a complicated Indian name that she mumbled in a high-pitched voice; she was covered with opulent rings and a robe, and she was overweight and looked worried. Nada insisted she sit beside him. Merrily he took hold of her big belly and shook it—twice, to be exact—laughing the second time.

"I must go on a diet," she said, in embarrassed falsetto, missing the point of his gesture, which I'm sure was just for fun, not judgment.

"You no raise hand, hand too heavy?" he said in a scolding tone, ribbing the woman who looked at him with pathetic confusion in her eyes. She was unable to grasp the idea that she was not bringing her hand up to her ear. It was simple, but she was deaf to his words because she was flustered and embarrassed.

"I'm very nervous. My mother's sick, and I'm always nervous anyway."

"Send your nervousness to Russia," Nada retorted. "Everybody come correct, whole world come correct—and not you? Why? You too!"

The poor woman was mortified, gaped seriously at him, and failed to see the light smile playing around his lips.

"Tala mean control—this way control everything. Seven notes, seven rishis, seven oceans, seven stars. Music is nature. Tala is god-alphabet.

Come correct now, then life correct. Walk, without any doubt. Know what you are doing!" He stopped and looked around at us as if to say, *Well?* He went on, "Everybody, time to come correct, all together! Here getting ticket to heaven, no birth, no death. Not come correct, no ticket—send back! Eighty-four million lives of dog-life and mud-world."

"This is all so new to me," the lady quavered pleadingly.

"Take the chance and do it now," Nada said, still trying to encourage her, and refusing to comply with the excuses she gave.

"I can't help it," she said.

"You can!" he insisted. He then told of a man he met in India, famous for his ability to write eighty-three letters on one particle of rice, several songs on the *edge* of a sheet of paper, and large portions of the Bhagavad Gita on a post card. The secret of this fantastic prowess of penmanship? Sadhana—that was the magic word. A training of the spiritual will, a project, a game, an experiment in creative consciousness.

After a while, Nada got the whole class chanting and counting together.

"Not know balance inside, nothing good, nothing happy."

That last remark caught my attention. Everything depended on being in tune with yourself. That came first, coming correct with everybody, and then everything else follows from that. To tune into the deeper, more creative part of yourself, it's a good idea to have some kind of self-forming practice, and some progress and enjoyment from working with the practice.

"One mind, different bodies here," he said, as we chanted in strict timing.

"No more man, no more woman, no more girl, no more boy, no more . . ." he trailed off.

I glanced around at our little group; together, as far as I could tell, we were all coming correct, including the squeaky man and the nervous woman.

17

Divine Detachment

ONE DAY ALIDA AND I TOOK our lesson together. We were a bit late arriving at the ashram. Nada began with a diatribe against a local musician who came to him for a lesson and who claimed to have studied tabla with Alla Rakha. He recounted and reenacted what he perceived to be the ineptness of the young musician.

"Very expert, no doubt," he said, "but no mind control." Nada always insisted on a sharp distinction between his special brand of mind control, in which he regarded himself as unsurpassed, and ordinary musical expertise, no matter how great. The old man's spirits were high, apparently content with his new surroundings at an ashram in upper New York state. He wanted to know if Alida and I were comfortable. We assured him that all was well. Later, on our walk, he asked that I take him to my room, which he ceremoniously scrutinized and approved of. He then asked to be shown Alida's room, which was upstairs in the woman's dormitory. I pointed, gently restraining him, and he nodded back.

"Little think," he said, laughing, and remarked how Parvati has caught him more than once making a *faux pas*.

"She better than me now," Nada said of his prize student who did in fact strike me as uncannily correct in her every gesture and remark; so much that sometimes I found it maddening. She never let a glance linger idly or a step pause without some purpose. Again Nada said that the young Californian was becoming his master. Come to think of it, once he forgot the name of the song he was teaching me. Humbly, he asked me for the first line.

"Will Parvati learn the *taans?*—the deeper secrets of nada yoga?" Alida asked, interrupting with a non sequitur.

Life was perpetual school for Nada, an everlasting series of tests: pass or get left back, graduation or rebirth in a pig's body. Learning was serious stuff.

"Time," he said, concerning Parvati learning the secrets of nada yoga.

"Finish, when I die, this art die. Not anyone ready. Now Parvati I teach, very nice. People in India I teach too. Longer than Parvati."

"So they didn't stay with you," I said.

"No, my agonist coming," he said, meaning to say antagonist, but by chance using an old Greek word for competitors and contestants.

"My disciples telling Nada Brahmananda—'don't know anything.'" He imitated the sound of bleating sheep.

"One disciple, sannyasi, throws up hands, fight me—Parvati knows this. These people, stonelike sitting—one mistake! Bow wow!" He barked, making his favorite sound suggesting perversity and "incorrectness."

"Everybody enjoy music, musician never enjoy, never change face— no joy—they want mistake, wait for mistake. 'Make joke,' they say, all musicians clapping, laughing." Their excessive competitiveness some- how spoiled their simple ability to enjoy the music they made.

"They clap when you make mistakes, but not when you come cor- rect," Alida remarked.

"Sitting silent like dead. Once back home many people program coming, many standing at the end. Everybody shake hand with me, everybody love—but musicians . . ." he stopped and made a comically rigid face, adding, "Everywhere this is true. Musician's heart is stone."

"I'm glad I'm no musician—I can enjoy everything you do," I said, in a genial outburst, but Nada's comment was more realistic. The spirit of competition can poison the ability to enjoy the music, and in fact tends to pervade all professions and much indeed that we do. There's a French word for this species of mental stuntedness—*ressentiment* (resentment).

"But you beginner now—you see, with another professor you also being like that!"

He had a point there, about academics. He smiled and remarked: "I'll tell you, this is nature. No musicians talk to me in New York City!"

I began to understand why Nada relished pummeling inept musicians who strayed onto his path. The revelation of his sense of not being respected by other musicians surprised me. I recalled reading a statement about him by the world-famous Ravi Shankar after listening to Nada perform: "I was impressed and touched." But this seemed to have been more the exception than the rule.

Nada seemed to be reliving some incidents in which he described how after a concert he was completely abandoned. In a way, I felt honored that Nada was comfortable enough with me and Alida to share his pique and chagrin.

"Everybody gone!" he said.

"And left you there?" Alida asked.

"Yah, sannyasi give troubles—yah, people give troubles," he added philosophically. Should we be surprised? It was Indian musicians and renunciants who gave him the hardest time.

We slipped into *raga bhairavi,* and I made a curious mistake in which everything came correct but in reverse. This caused Nada to bubble up with laughter, and he slapped me good-naturedly. Around Nada, failure was part of the fun. He made me feel I had all eternity to reach my goal. I tried to trick him into dropping the raga and getting on to the words of the song. When I mentioned *song* he broke out into enraptured song—"*ramanar . . .*" I reached for my pen and notebook. He stopped. *"Raga!"* he said. "Play raga!—you know, *raga bhupa,*" and suddenly he began to chant raga bhupa.

"I know that one," I said, trying to get him to come back.

Instead he ran through an exact review of everything we had done, going back to raga malakauns. Always the teacher, his method was to remind me that I had broken through previous barriers, and could do so again.

He played raga bhairavi with lightning speed several times, and urged me to do likewise. I just laughed, since I barely got it right slowly. It was new and strange to me. He quoted a Hindu proverb, *eka sada eka sabda,* which means, "if you get it once, you have it forever." Optimistic, I thought, but not realistic. The important stuff usually has to be drilled into me.

Never for one instant did Nada indulge in self-doubt. His words and acts had their origin in a place free from the shortcomings of ordinary mental life. In his company, it was almost easy to assume an attitude of divine optimism. Moreover, as I've often noticed, pessimism can sometimes be self-fulfilling.

"Ramanar bissara," he chanted, showing me the notes on the harmonium.

"What does that mean?"

In essence, his reply: the divine reality is the imperishable root of everything and that is the great thought to live by. It should be the lodestar of our attention, the one place to be anchored in. Everything else is constantly coming and going; what is up comes down, and the reverse—you become not you and something not you becomes you. That was the gist of what he was singing. There was an air of melancholy to this song.

He then lapsed into a prophetic riff, interpreting the song he was singing: "After, no electricity, no industry, no telephone, ocean come up,* nothing then, no office, no police, nothing—animals everywhere,

---

*I have to point out that after reading this phrase (in October, 2021) I read one of the direst reports describing how the rise of sea levels everywhere is going to cause havoc and destruction in coastal, sea-level regions planetwide.

tigers on Broadway, elephants and cobras on Fifth Avenue."

The song he was singing in the 1970s spoke uncannily to 2023 where climate turbulence is throwing the world into increasing disarray. The minstrel of things to come continued with his vision: "And man will be like that, naked, nothing—no cloth, ladies and gents; free, wild, with other animals—yes, like that!"

He made a curious comparison with the Hindenburg, which famously burst in flames and killed many: "Like 'plane' coming down, most die, some will live—God take care," he said, referring to the few survivors. It would be like that in the deluge and catastrophe to come. Most would die, he said, but the world would somehow be clean and young again. The coming catastrophes would plant seeds for a new form of consciousness.

"When this Earth up down going, God take care people," he said in summary.

"What does *bissara* mean?" one of us asked.

"Ramanar bissara—God's name never end." Our fortunes are always changing, as long as we're fixated on the external world, which itself is always changing. He paused and cheerfully added: "Twenty years before, very beautiful; now getting old, old, old. Every hour, change. Going down, down, down!" he said, intoning the word *down,* making a mantra of it, almost making it sound beautiful.

And again we broke into laughter. His portrayal of the grim vicissitudes of life and our future on Earth became funny. What's to do but sing the nullity of money, life, love, whatever comes and goes? For Nada it was all one, all empty, and only song abides.

"Ismenha na kou cha sara bunda, nothing is certain, Earth gone, sea come"—prescient, for as the Earth warms the seas are rising as the glaciers and Antarctica are melting four times faster than any time in the past. His mind then jumped: "We are all coming here, July fourth, a million people all together. Celebration, all year getting ready—fourth finished—all gone home."

So, life is preparing for a celebration, which comes and goes abruptly, and sends us all back home to ordinary existence, caught up in the endless round dance of death and rebirth. This is grim realism, but there is some good news: there is an option that may help us achieve happiness. The one task in life is to surrender to the Infinite Mind. Name and think of it as you will—it is one of the great and recurrent memes of human spirituality.

Nada's mood was merry. "Alone!" he said, and laughed. In the end, we have to rely on our ourselves. "Be ye lamps unto yourselves," said the Buddha.

A stark but accurate picture of our embodied existence. And yet, the more he chanted this vision of catastrophe and loneliness, the calmer and lighter I felt.

"You see and enjoy—finish, not attach—yes, enjoy," he said vigorously, "but not attach." "But that's hard," Alida said. "The more you enjoy, the more you get attached."

He nodded in assent to Alida's observation, but continued with his preachment: "From anyone good bad you hear—forget—not bother either way." He was still commenting on the song he was teaching. He was saying not to be overwhelmed by the responses you elicit from people, whether good or bad. Then he remarked about words. "Words not killing you—words are air."

Yes and no, in my opinion. Words of plain fools may be just air we can afford to ignore. But the words of fools in government and business and religion cannot be dismissed so easily. They need to be taken seriously, and countered. In the next chapter we'll have a look at the way Nada willed himself beyond the language of ordinary life.

18

Anestehan,
the Way to Power

PEOPLE OFTEN REPORTED THAT after listening to Nada sing, a pain or sickness they may have had would disappear; the songman, though, was reluctant to take credit for healing anyone. He was unsympathetic to a passive approach to healing. He would have disliked the word *patient*. Instead, he offered his students the means to heal themselves, his model of self-healing being the yoga of music. He told me a story about a boy who stuttered.

"This eight-year-old boy, very lovely, can't talk right, unhappy. Mother bring boy to ashram. Mother take lesson. One day, mother cry. 'Why you cry?' I say. 'People laughing at my boy—stutter. Doctors not help.'"

The boy was normal but for his speech impediment; afraid to talk, he would stutter if he tried, so he remained silent most of the time.

"I told her, 'Bring your boy here.' 'He not want come, everybody laughing.' 'Bring boy,' I told her, 'nobody laughing here.' When he came, I told everyone not to laugh. I gave him some little cake to eat. I, not talk, nothing."

Nada took care not to force the boy into the position of having to speak; at the same time, he occupied the boy's mouth with the more pleasant task of eating some cake.

"Mother's teaching time, she made mistakes," Nada resumed.

"That boy understand. I teaching one, two, three, four—when mother making mistake, boy—*hmm . . . hmm*—he know. Two, three days I teaching; always that boy coming with mother. One day, I stop—now *you* do, I tell the boy. One, two . . ." Nada intoned very slowly and rhythmically.

"Not stutter," he said, and again he began to count very slowly and rhythmically, gradually doubling and doubling the pace and switching to the Sanskrit syllables. The effect was extraordinarily soothing; it was easy to see how the boy's speech impediment might well have diminished. After a few days, the boy was doing better than his mother, and before long Nada had the erstwhile shy boy singing in a program with him.

"Father and sister and many people came to this program. And everybody very happy. Now the boy is going to school. When I had to leave, he cried. 'I'm coming with you,' he said. 'Later,' I tell him. First, growing a little; then come. Very difficult now."

The discussion turned to the use of vibrations in the art of self-healing—wordless vibrations that echo the notes of the raga. First the notes are sung, *sa ri ga . . .* then *ah ah ah. . . .* Every song begins this way, with a melodic pattern, or raga, and then the taan. Every song is preceded by a long internal vibration, barely audible and puzzling to the uninitiated listener. This silent mental act is said to vibrate in the etheric (imaginal) plane, creating, he once said, a playground for the celestials.

Nada's method was to begin with an internal repetition of the taan and gradually make the vibrations audible. The song materializes from the depths of one's inward being. Every song Nada sang was a ritual reenactment of creation, the manifestation of his inward being in the shape of sounds in the air.

"What is the connection between taans and kundalini?" I asked.

"You see," Nada replied, grasping my question immediately, "each of the chakras I control everyday during my sadhana. Called kundalini taans. Experiment, three men hold me—vibration coming here!" He pointed to his lower spine.

"But can this vibration be *heard?* Could you perform this for an audience?" I asked. He replied to my question at once, a hint of indignation in his voice.

"Yes, heard, *microphone*—coming public!"

Nada's chief musical "instrument" was his body; his life was the raw material of this sacred art. Perfection of his art work was the means to perfection of his life.

The discussion turned to breath-control: "How are you able to hold your breath for thirty-five minutes?"

"You know swimming?" he responded instantly.

"Yes," I said.

"You go under water? Yes?"

"Yes," I said, not getting what he was driving at.

"What doing underwater?"

Still perplexed, I said nothing, and he repeated the question.

"I stop breathing," I said this time.

"How you able?" he said.

"I just stop."

"Automatic—khumbaka doing, automatic—no sense, no thinking, death-body."

Doing khumbaka was like dying; Nada's daily practice of khumbaka was a practice of dying. But it wasn't really automatic at all. Living and breathing are automatic; to suspend one's breath for thirty-five minutes is anything but automatic. Khumbaka, which takes practice, was a transcendent gesture—like throwing down the gauntlet before nature.

He mentioned others he had witnessed in India perform similar feats of breath control—men who bury themselves twelve feet under the earth in a box. Under cement, no air, nothing, he said.

"Day and night, police watch—eight days!"

"This you don't do automatically," I said. "It takes practice, is much practice necessary?"

"Eh!" he moaned, "many years!"

"By the way," I said, "was the man still alive after eight days?"

"Yes, police there, find him living!"

I wanted to know if there were any special techniques he employed to evolve his unusual powers.

"Yes," he replied, "once, one hundred eight days, special practice. *Anestehan* called that one. I not come out, not see sun."

Nada described a retreat he underwent at one point in his career, a retreat of one hundred eight days whose purpose it was to master the taan and nadakhumbaka—which, it should be remembered, is more than just a period of prolonged breath retention; for while he holds his breath, and in that sense becomes a "death-body," he is also unblinkingly gazing upon his icon and performing complex rhythms with his drums.

"Inside, no food, one hundred eight days. One small window; each day a man came, and gave a little milk. Arrangement, government and me. I talk with no one, see no one, one hundred eight days. Small room near ashram. I practice every day, day and night."

"What was the purpose of this?" I asked. I had heard of jazz musicians retreating to places of seclusion—they call it "wood-shedding"—but never of anything so extreme. Nada's anestehan was a fast combined with sensory deprivation—and for one hundred eight days?

"Anestehan means getting siddhis. Many people ask, 'What you doing? Why stay in dark? You might die.' People say, 'Don't do this!' But I die anyway one day. Must do this. Succeed or die," he flatly pronounced.

"But not talking to anyone, not eating—didn't you go a little crazy?"

"No," he said, looking surprised, "that is anestehan, getting siddhis." He explained to me that since he was driven from his life in Mysore and forced into making vows of renunciation, he was determined to do what was needed to master the vibration yoga. That had become his sole desire. He would keep it up for the appointed 108 days, or die. Then he explained how the latter might have come about: "Someday you not hear sound—mean die."

If they stopped hearing him practice in his cell, they'd know he was dead.

"There always police, twenty-four hours. Inside, no telephone call, no dogs barking, no children crying. One hundred and eight days, good sadhana time. Came very successful; master now taans, nadakhumbaka. And after, government research me, test my body."

"You broke through."

"I not see sun. One day you not stay."

"Amazing—normally you'd begin to hallucinate," I remarked. I asked if, at any time during his retreat, he saw things, images, sounds that weren't there. Apparently not.

Nada jumped to another topic. There was a very rough man—some uptight functionary at the ashram in Rishikesh—who felt Nada was not working enough. The man imagined music was all play. Nada offered to pay the disgruntled fellow eight hundred rupees if he would do *his* work for eight hours. The very rough man accepted the challenge, no doubt thinking it would be easy and profitable. Nada taught him a song.

"Yes, I do, I do," the man sat and managed to survive two hours. But that was all he could manage. "I surrender," he said, "keep your eight hundred rupees, I not do this work."

"What were you thinking all those days inside that dark room?" I persisted, still curious to catch a glimpse of what he was feeling during anestehan.

"I take God's name, do *japa,*" he said without ceremony, "same way Sai Baba got power; by long sadhana."

I asked him again what he was thinking and feeling; maybe I wanted to hear of demons and temptations assaulting him, moments of madness, self-rending doubt, the torments of loneliness. But there was nothing of the sort. Again he jumped to another subject. He talked of Parvati's struggles with sadhana; she cried and became angry. But such were no longer issues for him, he wanted me to understand. He never cried or got angry.

"You professor—also practice," he said, emphasizing that practice was the secret of any pursuit of excellence. I began to wonder what the philosophical equivalent of anestehan would be.

"Yes," I assented. "I practice. But not for a one hundred eight day fast underground in a dark room. I'd go out of my mind."

"This is not your aim. I am sannyasi. I told you. I die, or finish."

His resolve to die or succeed freed him from all the customary obstacles. Indifferent to remaining on the planet, there was nothing to prevent him from projecting his whole being into a superhuman task. The darkness and solitude were already like death. There was nothing to capture his attention or distract him from his goal.

"You do khumbaka every day now?"

"Every day—this one item took seven years to master. But now every day."

Parvati said it was a tonic, physical and spiritual, and essential to his supernormal health. Nada looked up at me with a penetrating glance.

"I not want life," he said once more, undramatically.

"You're not afraid of death at all. Many people *say* they don't fear death. . . ."

"People worry," he said and paused. "I never worry. Vishnu, very important man no doubt, thinking about all centers, all people; day and night—but also worry!" Clear was the difference between Nada and Vishnu, who advertised himself with a photo doing a headstand on the ledge of a New York skyscraper.

To illustrate our dogged attachment to life and to things, Nada told of an uncle he once saw die. This uncle had hidden the family fortune in the house somewhere. In India the practice was not to rely on banks but to stash money away in a secret place. The dying man's son was pleading with his father to reveal the whereabouts of the hidden money and other family valuables. At length, a cow—a sacred beast in India that roams free—wandered into the room of the dying man and proceeded to chew upon a broomstick. This incensed Nada's uncle, and he cried out that his son was neglecting to care for his property, outraged by the sight of the chewed-up broomstick. In the midst of this petulant outburst, the upset uncle died on the spot.

"He died not taking God's name!" Nada laughed as he described the absurd death of his uncle, who worried more about a cow chewing on a broomstick than the momentous event of his own demise. Whether the hidden fortune was ever found, Nada couldn't say, but then he said:

"Parvati always saying, 'Swamiji—go to doctor, check-up getting! But I not want doctor. Never go."

"You don't care?" I said.

"No," he said.

"But that's also because you're healthy."

"People like life too much," Nada calmly observed.

"Yes," I agreed, "it's an instinct—one-sided, maybe. Speaking for myself, I'm warmly attached to my life. I guess I'll have to work on that."

19

The Man
Who Never Dreams

FOR THREE NIGHTS IN A ROW, scientists of the University of Ottawa wired Nada up to test for his dream cycles and REM sleep. The results were astonishing: there was no evidence of dream sleep.

"Not one," Nada said.

"Second night, third night, same—wires! I sleeping, doctors sitting there, watching. Wake up, not one dream!"

"What did the doctors say about this, Swamiji?"

"One big doctor come. 'When Swami came here, we test him three days; no dreams.' And then, surprised, he came and asks me, 'Why you not dream?'"

"And what did you say?"

"I said: before, doctor, you never saw Nada Brahmananda, never saw my face, my body—and never think. Now, see all this, thinking, and from thinking, dreams coming. Before, never see, never dreaming."

"Or," he continued, shifting his example, "you I saw, and you saw me; you think, but I not think, finish—no dreaming—finish."

So Nada's experiences leave no strong emotional traces in his mind. This would seem to assume that none of the people Nada ever meets, and none of his external perceptions, ever produce any memorable effects. Without a memory trace, there is no material for him to work up into a dream. Moreover, just as he has no dreams, there is no unfinished business to motivate him to reincarnate after death. I suppose this is a possible explanation of Nada never dreaming.

Nada then tried to explain that all his life he slept very little; however, this would not normally eliminate the need to dream. It might in fact cause him to need to dream even more.

"I understand what you say, Swamiji," I said, "still this is strange: people, not dreaming, not sleeping, get sick—but you're healthy."

Parvati suggested that yogis enjoy a qualitatively deeper type of sleep, which might account for the absence of any signs of dreaming with Nada.

Nada added that he catches a wink or two when teaching and students are performing correctly. It happened with me once, so I knew that was true.

"Mistake, wake up!" he said, opening his eyes with sudden alarm.

I asked if he saw anything during these transient naps, images or pictures in his mind. Nothing at all, he exclaimed.

"Swamiji, one time you told me you used to dream, but always the same dream that you are giving a big musical program," Parvati said, suddenly remembering.

"Yes," he recalled, "there, maharaja palace, staying, wonderful. Beds also you never see like that. Wonderful. And sleeping that time, I dream!"

"What a single-minded man," I said. "I've never known a man more one-minded, totally at one with himself."

This seemed to attest to Nada's theory of dreaming. As you think, so you dream. Of course, the modern theory is that we dream what we don't think, or what we tend to shut out from our conscious thinking. It's called repression. Incredibly, it would seem that Nada represses nothing; or, to put it another way, against all odds, he manages to be at one with himself all the time. He sings in his waking world and he sings in his dream world. In all worlds Nada is at one with the divine song within himself.

Parvati agreed on the point about Nada's single-mindedness and explained how people often request his presence and performance, at different programs and he refuses whenever possible.

"I told them," he said, "my life is different. I have no interest. My ashram in Rishikesh, same; these people, anything doing, I never come. No committee, no meeting, I never go. No matter what is happening— no matter how big, how important—*I don't want it!*"

Talk about dropping out! Nada's will was iron-like. He simply made up his mind and refused to get involved in the debilitating red-tape of mundane existence.

"One time," he continued, "seventy-nine, my birthday, that day, everybody give blessing. Many swamis give blessing and give lecture on my birthday. Krishnananda start. Wonderful man! 'Swami Nada Brahmananda coming every year young, we are coming old! Why is this?' 'I never think—income tax, sales tax'—everybody laughing. People always thinking! Thinking makes you dull," he said, bubbling up with soft laughter from inside.

"Every day, thousand letters coming in," he went on, referring to the stress and strain important swamis like Swami Vishnu, trying to save the world, must undergo. "Government risk, income tax risk, personal problem, worry, people every day fighting! Many program all year round. Many people coming there, kings come, presidents come—I never going, never. Never see anyone, only class or satsang. Full mind singing together, learning together." He paused and smiled at me. "No singing and learning! Then I say, 'Goodbye, ladies and gents!'"

We grew silent. Parvati closed her eyes and rolled her head rhythmically. A breeze blew the door open and sounds of chanting below floated up the stairway. I got up and closed the door. It was hot and muggy and my body felt heavy. I decided to accept the heaviness—useless to have a fighting attitude against the whims of the weather. I retraced what I just did in my mind; I put more into it than needed. Add up a thousand wasted small efforts a day, a thousand pointless mind spasms, and "what you getting?" A shriveled horizon, according to Nada, as well as premature decrepitude.

Nada then told me of a time he performed for the first president of India, a man apparently weighed down by much thinking, Jawaharlal Nehru. "He sitting stonelike," Nada began, with hushed intensity. "Yes, President silent. Everybody see him, also silent. I very feel. After, I sing *sado mana kano*—ego, leave, useless. One simple rule: happiness, unhappiness you think same. Getting insult, getting respect, you think same. . . ."

"You sang this song for the first President of India?"

"Yes," he said.

The song he sang apparently melted the very stonelike President Nehru, who began to display some emotion, and this was followed in like manner by members of his retinue. The allotted forty-minute recital swelled into a marathon three-hour performance.

He was shunting back and forth from commenting on the song and illustrating from his own experience. Speaking of Parvati, he said, "Anybody give insult, she feel—not me." I had come to see that this team of spiritual minstrels was having some bumpy times, and that it was especially hard for the master's consort.

Nada's point was to demonstrate how "practical" indifference to opposites was. I took him to mean "don't get altogether carried away by anything, good or bad." The best thing is serene acceptance, no matter what fate doles out to us; there is something in us higher than fate. He told me he felt nothing on occasions when he was snubbed by inferior musicians and that he felt nothing special when he was acknowledged and wildly applauded for his performances. It was all the same to the celestial songman, so in tune with himself that he never dreamed.

20

Nadakhumbaka on Paradise Island

THIS HAPPENED IN THE Bahamas in 1979. It was still early in the day and it turned out to be the last time I would be with Nada. He would soon be returning to the ashram in the Himalayas. I had come not for a lesson but for a last listen and a last chance to talk with him. The chanting began haltingly and I could see the duo didn't quite have it together yet. Then Nada glanced at Parvati and began to drum in earnest. Bit by bit new listeners wandered in under the green and white-striped canopy that swelled and swayed with the wind, and the singers began to sound their song with fuller and steadier cadence.

Before long the audience was deeply entranced and the Caribbean afternoon was vibrant with sounds of a raga garland. Nada's face noticeably brightened when Sant Keshavadas appeared, and he inserted the name of his fellow musician into the lyrics of the raga, a tribute to a soul-brother. We were all pretty much carried away on a wave of lovely feeling. It was a lazy afternoon and there was no fanfare leading up to the chanting, but when the raga ended the audience burst into applause, a reflex from the rush of good spirits we had all imbibed.

Nada remarked to the audience that in India women were not taught sacred music, then paused and nodded at Parvati who bowed slightly but not shyly. The old monk said he saw no sense in this exclusion of women. He thought women's liberation by means of music was a great idea.

"If mother gives us life, why not learn sacred music?" he asked. He noted that in India musicians either drum or sing but that Parvati did both. I smiled at the thought of a California gal making waves in mystic India!

His spirits raised now, the master of breath and intellect said he would offer a sample of nadakhumbaka. He invited a man from the audience who was wearing a T-shirt with an image of his wife and family emblazoned on it, who happened to be a physician from Maine, to check if there was any glue on a silver dollar he held in his hand.

"No glue?" asked Nada, asking for confirmation in a manner faintly mocking the scientific investigator.

"No glue," agreed the physician.

The physician was then requested to stroke the perfectly bald pate of the mirthful sannyasi. This was done with care, and it was further confirmed that no trace of glue could be found. A picture of dancing Shiva was placed on a dais before him. Then he got into an erect posture, placed the silver dollar on his head, quickly and without the slightest hesitation drew a breath, and thus commenced, slowly, and in rhythm with all our hearts, to beat upon the tabla.

This he did for exactly twenty-four minutes on a single breath, unblinkingly, beating out endlessly subtle and exciting rhythms on the drums, his attention riveted on an image of the dancing god of destruction and resurrection. All of us present seemed to lapse into profound meditation, sharing somehow in his perfect suspension of the breath of life. He took a breath prematurely, I later learned, because something was tickling his throat and he had the urge to cough, so he only lasted twenty-four minutes (thirty-five minutes was the typical duration of this exercise). When people spoke in wonder concerning this feat, he always shrugged it off. Anybody can do it with practice, he would say.

On April 21, Ravi Shankar and Alla Rakha arrived on Paradise Island for an evening performance of spiritual ragas rarely heard. There was a general feeling that this was the peak event of the week—and every nook and cranny of audience space would be filled. All afternoon the carpenters were buzzing about with their electric saws. Ravi Shankar insisted on having an extra platform built and placed on the stage, which apparently was not high enough for him.

I hadn't seen much of Nada for a day and wondered if he would seclude himself from the fanfare of the evening performance, thinking he might have felt slighted by the relatively poor role he had been given during the week. I was wrong. For when the music began later that evening I found Nada right up front clapping in rhythm with Alla Rakha, and with such exuberance that Shambu Das, a pupil of Ravi Shankar, had to quiet him down.

I hardly caught a glimpse of Nada during the remaining day or so. Once I noticed him from a short distance, standing in the sun before his little green cottage.

He waved to me, smiled and inquired: "You happy?"

I nodded and waved back. And that was the last time I saw the celestial songman. Happy? Yes, I'm happy to have kept a record of some exchanges I had with this remarkable man, a living exponent of the ancient Indian art and science of musical vibrations. I'm left with a trove of ideas that invite further exploration. What follows are some thoughts and tentative conclusions, in which we can reflect a little on a few of the deeper meanings of music.

21

Reflections on Transcendental Music

THE TRANSCENDENTAL FACTOR

Some time has gone by since that last glimpse I had of Swami Nada, and his kindly question, Was I happy? I remember Nada as a figure of rare musical abilities of a spiritual type, and also a man with some strange powers, powers he always said he acquired by means of an almost superhuman focus of attention; powers, he said, that were in principle available to us all, depending on how much of ourselves we're willing to invest.

Since I first recorded my experiences with Nada Brahmananda, my curiosity about extraordinary human capacities has not abated. I have further explored the lives of people with transcendental powers, for example, Joseph of Copertino.[1] There is a large body of mystical and paranormal phenomena, often well documented; it's largely ignored and played down by the mainstream scientific culture. This is not surprising in light of the way science has evolved, with its bias toward materialism, along with the Protestant Reformation, with its own bias against miracles.[2]

In spite of these downbeat trends, people everywhere continue to have extraordinary experiences, some of which qualify as miracles, and clearly expand our idea of human potential. For one thing, the available data point to a new paradigm of the mind-body relationship, which we can only touch on here. The phenomena speak to expanded mental capacities, at a time of unprecedented need for new ways of thinking. In my view, human potential may be an especially crucial concept in light of the unprecedented climate crisis it is presently being forced to confront. The message from the scientists who know what they're talking about is that we have about ten years grace to come together as a species if we hope to recover from the climate chaos we have inflicted on the planet. No matter what we do, say the experts, it will take at least three decades before we might conceivably return to life as we once knew it. But to avoid the worst catastrophic outcomes, we humans will have to radically change how we live. These changes will demand a mode of life that is, in some ways, the diametric opposite of how many of us live today, especially the wealthiest and the most comfortable.

This crisis *could* ignite the greatest cultural and spiritual renaissance of human history. Given the existential challenge, we might come together as a species and do what needs to be done to save ourselves. The challenge is being forced upon us by something we cannot fully control and that leaves none of us safe or secure, though, as usual, the poor and the powerless will surely suffer the most.

So how then does music figure in this existential drama of life on Earth? Music—in the arts, science, and religion—speaks to new forms of consciousness. And it is new forms of consciousness above all that we need to change our way of life. A new, music-inspired paradigm of consciousness would be about restoring harmony with the natural world. Instead of treating the natural, living world around us as if its sole purpose were to provide resources for human consumption, pleasure, and profitability, we will need to recapture a more indigenous sense of being part of a living planet and of being stewards of its life-giving powers and mysteries. Consciousness at large needs a reckoning of human crimes against nature and indigenous peoples; against the extinction of plants and animals occurring a hundred times faster than ever before; against the destruction of lifeways, arts, languages, and spiritual ideas categorized as "savage" or "primitive." To avoid the results of the long, thoughtless abuse of Gaia, our terrestrial ecosphere, we will have to awaken to new ideas and values and have the courage to dispense with certain entrenched ideas and values.

Great myths have been spun from ideas about the mystical powers of music; the story of Orpheus and Eurydice, for example, is long-lasting in myth and legend. Orpheus, son of the King of Thrace and the Muse Calliope, became master of the seven-stringed lyre, which Apollo taught him. His music, songs, and poetry exerted supernatural power over men and women, and over animals and plants and stones.

But grief was his fate when his beloved wife, Eurydice, in flight from the advances of Aristaeus, was bitten by a snake in the grass and died. Orpheus, in desperation, followed her to Hades and, with the help of his lyre, persuaded the king of death to allow her to return to life. The favor was granted on condition that he not look back at Eurydice as she followed him from the underworld. In his anxiety, however, he did look back, causing her to vanish, and thus die a second time. Orpheus became the symbol of the quest for immortality; as master of transcendental music, he is associated with being near death.[3]

Nada Brahmananda told us of tigers and cobras who were among his chief fans, but also his friends whom he personally fed and took into his living space. He tamed the animals with his music and his friendliness. Harmony is one of the powers of music, and as well a Platonic ideal and Jungian archetype. Music is also a metaphor for various types of *subtle* harmony, including the social, political, and aesthetic. All human relationships are based on subtle complexes of emotional harmonics. Immersing ourselves in the harmonics of music, perhaps we can learn more deeply to harmonize with living nature and with each other.

We may have to learn ways of talking to nature just as children, poets, and mystics do, through symbols, images, and songs. Success in this venture requires that we learn to reanimate our perception of nature and of each other.

James Hillman, of Jungian persuasion, recommended personification as a way of restoring soul to our conversation with the world at large. To do this we have to exploit the magical power of language. The key is being less literal minded and more freely metaphoric in how we verbalize reality. There is more to the word *fire* than a number of degrees on the Fahrenheit scale. Addiction to literal mindedness is the enemy of the active power of imagination.[4]

My experience and the results of research into the authentically inexplicable leave me certain of gargantuan gaps of ignorance in myself and in the mainstream scientific outlook. All the gaps of knowledge are exciting challenges to science. More interestingly, however, they are also challenges to each of us, personally, raising questions about the unknown scope of our human capacities and possible experience. According to the reductionist cliché, we are stardust. Sure, but with one correction: we are *conscious* stardust, which implies a more animated story.

I began this book with a story about music and an unidentified aerial intelligence that engaged with me and two other people. The message felt like some weird affirmation of spiritual music, linking John Coltrane and the dome of Our Lady of Pompey in Greenwich Village to a musically hip Light Intelligence from the outer space of the Unknown. It certainly appeared like an external intelligence that was communicating with us. But who or what was behind the message remains a mystery.

Today we have entered a new stage of the story. Finally, starting in 2017, the government and military personnel have admitted that something keeps penetrating our air space that dances around and even seems to joke with our technology, and nobody has any idea of where it's coming from or what it is. The unidentified aerial phenomena (UAPs) apparently like to tease and play games with our multi-million-dollar jet planes. They seem immune to the constraints of gravity and physical space; there are reports of people being levitated when in close contact with UAPs.

Reports of levitation occur more frequently in the context of intense religious experiences. St. Joseph of Copertino taking to the air was invariably preceded by him lapsing into a state of ecstasy. It was also repeatedly observed that he would emit a frightening scream at the moment he took off. What is it about the ecstastic state that enabled his body to transcend gravity? I found that almost all saints and yogis who levitated did so in this uniquely altered state of consciousness.[5]

Swami Nada Brahmananda's practical philosophy and unusual abilities were grounded in what we might call an ecstatic lifestyle—detached, focused, disposed in thought and behavior toward losing himself in transcendent reality, most of all when musically evoked in the ragas he lived and sang. Ecstasy implies being outside your normal mental self, which seems to allow for the influx of the force that makes levitation possible—a mind swept clean of all content is a mind made receptive to transcendent force.

We're pondering the idea of transcendental music, an archetypal configuration and wide-ranging symbol as well as an actual auditory experience, heard sometimes in dreams or through supernormal auditions. Swami Nada opened me to an expanded view of what music is and what it may yet become. People everywhere generally like music of one kind or another, and many love music, making it their profession or their spiritual practice, or listening, cultivating, and cherishing it greatly.

There is also a type of musical experience with properties that transcend the gamut of familiar emotions: states of ineffable joy in which one claims to know and feel oneself to be immortal. I recall a conversation with Laura Dale, for many years the esteemed editor of the

American Journal of Psychical Research. Laura got into this controversial field because of her interest in evidence for postmortem survival. This was personal to Laura; she lost the love of her life when he was a young musician. Knowing she was familiar with the best evidence for life after death, I asked her once what her feelings were about the reality of an afterworld, well-acquainted with the subject as she was.

Her reply surprised me. "You know," she said, "I'll tell you what convinces me of immortality—listening to Beethoven's *Missa Solemnis.*" Listening to the music, she said, put her in a mental space where she felt perfectly happy to die, knowing it would be as easy as stepping through an open door into a new world. She couldn't imagine the music she heard coming from anything less than immortality.

Beyond all the evidence she was acquainted with—mediumship, hauntings, apparitions of the dead, reincarnation studies—great music inspired her to believe that her lost lover might have survived. So there are powers of music that can alter and enlarge our visceral sense of reality. Many have found it to be so, and Swami Nada seemed to embody this feature of transcendental music, which he always associated with a living divine reality.

The latent powers of music, according to Indo-Tibetan traditions, range from the paranormal to the mystical. With Nada Brahmananda as our point of departure, we can track the idea of a higher kind of music. To begin with, music and life itself have something deeply in common: air and breath, without which we can neither live nor sing or make any kind of music. Music is made of sound that is made of vibrations of air. Air is the matrix of music and of life; we die without the air we breathe and without air the world would be as silent as a tomb. The Greek word for breath or air is *psyche* and the Latin word for moving air or wind is *spiritus*. In music we seem to draw upon the breath and spirit of life itself. And since it is mind and feeling that shape and indeed create the forms of music, we can think of music as one of the more perfect examples of the marriage of mind and matter.

Nada's phenomena were studied by scientists outside of India. I was struck by reports of three days at Ottawa University in which it was concluded that Nada had no dream life. Nada told me that he slept no more than two hours a night. And yet the man lived for ninety-seven years, reportedly in perfect health in all his days. Mind control, Nada's major motto, was also evident to a group of political and spiritual leaders once at a conference in the Bahamas. In a strange performance, before his distinguished audience, the Swami proved mastery over his body by consciously raising his blood pressure to 240. All the indications point to an extraordinary potential based on the ability to use the vibrations of music and breath control to animate and energize the body in ways we have yet to fully understand or appreciate.

Swami Nada is discussed at length in a book published in 1966 by Alfonso Caycedo, M.D., titled *India of Yogis*. Dr. Caycedo spent years studying and interviewing the Indian and Tibetan yogis in their ashrams and cave retreats in a one-hundred and fifty mile stretch around the Himalayas. His focus was on the psychophysical dimension of the various yogas and their bearing on mental and physical health. The doctor was very interested in Swami Nada and wrote of him: "If a man can be called a phenomenon, Swami Nada Brahmananda is one." Nada had supernormal control of key bodily functions, obtained by means of his musical practice, such that, as Dr. Caycedo put it: "One might say that his body is a musical instrument, and he can play on any part of it, like a musician." One wonders if the image of a body being transformed into a musical instrument points to a type of potential existing in us all. As to Nada's strange abilities, he added: "As an occidental doctor, I can freely vouchsafe that I have myself verified, checked it all, and the vibrations were, in fact, felt wherever these had been directed." Numerous photos in the book illustrate Nada's projected vibrations being recorded on different parts of his body, for example, at the crown of his head or by his ear.[6]

Nada yoga is ancillary to bhakti yoga, the yoga of devotion and ecstatic love. Nada's vibrations then are oriented around the idea of divine love. The hymns and ragas (melodies) were always stepping-stones toward amity and divine union. That union was the soul of his message and guided his teaching with great single-mindedness. In the chapter on Krishna's Flute, he explained how my flute was an instrument for sublimating my discordant emotions into new harmonies and self-transcendence.

At the deepest level, nada yoga is about refining the quality of our awareness such that we can hear what Kabir called the "unstruck" sound (*anahat*): the mystic chord of the inmost heart, the unheard melody, the ineffable voice of God. It is a sound, a vibe, that lifts us beyond our daily boilerplate perceptions. All the senses have their higher forms. There are physical lights we see with our eyes, and there are illuminations of spirit in whose presence we are sometimes spiritually transformed. Annekatrin Puhle collected and analyzed eight hundred experiences of transcendental light.[7] What is striking is the great variety of circumstances in which people undergo these illuminations. Almost invariably, in some positive way, they change lives. Perhaps the best-known example would be the "Being of Light" that people who have near-death experiences often say they meet and meld with.

Notice the analogy with sound. There is music we hear with our ears and there are sounds of surpassing beauty we may hear without any known physical source (see below). For every sense we possess, we have a transcendental version of that sense. Another example would be widespread accounts of the odor of sanctity among mystics, yogis, and ecstatics.[8] The ordinary memory we possess has a transcendental counterpart, as in cases of people near death who report seeing their entire lives flash before them in a sweeping panoramic recollection. The experience of one's whole life passing before you at great speed is like the music heard in cases of near-death, often sounding like a chorus of countless voices, reverberating all together, *super-harmoniously*.

MUSIC AND THE KALI YUGA

Nada believed in the reality of the Kali Yuga; he also believed that music was the best medicine for people suffering from the evils of the age. The age of *Kali* is an age of *conflict,* not quite the same as Kali, the goddess of death and time. Music, it is said, is our best spiritual ally for coping with this deadly duo.

What, then, is the healing remedy of music? One feature of music seems obvious: harmony, which is the opposite of conflict. The word *harmony* is rich in meanings. The Oxford English Dictionary gives this definition: "Combination or adaptation of parts, elements, or related things, so as to form a consistent and orderly whole; agreement, accord, congruity." More specifically, in music: "Harmony is the simultaneous sounding of several notes, and includes concords and discords." That is, counterpoint may be part of harmony. Both of these definitions of harmony encompass a range of connotations that take us beyond the circle of literal music. The deeper harmonies of all life, of body and soul, of person and nature, are part of the deepest, most inward, and most subtle music. We need to wend our way in that direction of subtle music, toward harmony between body and soul, and between us humans and the entire natural world that we depend on for our life.

Alain Daniélou, musician and great scholar of Indian religion, stresses the antiquity of Indian music, its spiritual and scientific value, and its relationship to language. *Nada* he defines as "intelligible sound," sound imbued with myth and meaning. Music is a story, a metaphysical language; a voice that speaks to us from millennia of vibrant traditions.[9]

Indian music distinguishes two kinds of sound: one, a vibration of air; the other, a vibration of ether, not perceptible to normal hearing, but which is said to be "the principle of manifestation." The ether is not a reputable concept in today's physics. The ether was deemed an occult substance assumed to be weightless, transparent, frictionless, undetectable chemically or physically, and literally permeating all matter and space. To my ears, the description of the rejected notion of ether is a good description of mind. I would suggest the psychokinetic imagination was the "principle of manifestation," the power of the mind to manifest physical effects, like levitation, or healing, or fragrance, or transcendental music, or materialization and dematerialization,and so on.

As I read it, the Indian theory of music is based on the primacy of creative mind and takes us back to the metaphysics of the Upanishads, and the psychophysics of Patanjali's Yoga Aphorisms. Edward Kelly and Ian Whicher note in "Patanjali's Yoga Sutras and the Siddhis" that Patanjali stresses the idea that *samyama,* or intense concentration of attention, is the key variable responsible for the production of siddhis or paranormal phenomena. Patanjali's work "presents an explicit, elaborate, and testable theoretical statement of relationships between mystical states and supernormal phenomena."[10] So extraordinary music is one example of widely reported empirical findings that connect altered mental states with certain types of supernormal phenomena. This empirical connection has hugely significant experimental implications.

The etymology of the word *nada* is intriguing: Alain Daniélou notes that the syllable *na* means "breath" and *da* means "fire of intellect." The union of breath and the fire of intellect is the core meaning of Nada, a more poetic rendering of "intelligible sound." In the *Sangita Bhashya,* we find this panegyric: Nada is the treasure of happiness for the happy, the distraction of those who suffer, the first messenger of the god of love. . . . It is the fifth approach to the Eternal Wisdom."[11] That is a pretty high ranking for the potential value of music.

Daniélou writes at length about the Kali Yuga and, like our Swami, is a firm believer in the Indian endtime scenario. Danielou tells us we're in the "twilight" of the Kali age, in short, very close to the end of the current cycle of human existence. According to the Indian calendar, we entered this twilight in 1939—the nub of the Second World War. Unfortunately, it seems we are now at the end of the twilight and facing the night of the world. A radical conflict is playing out between humans and the entire natural world of water, air, and earth, a mostly unconscious and, ultimately, suicidal conflict. Music, rightly understood and practiced, would be a way to reconnect with the living nature we depend on for our existence. The fault is in our undeveloped ear for the vital harmonics of Nature, preoccupied as we are with plundering and exploiting nature for its resources, defined in terms of human benefits, to the exclusion of the ecosphere as a whole. This is clearly the way to eco-suicide.

HINTS OF THINGS TO COME FROM SOCRATES AND EURIPIDES

Was there something wrong from the start with the classical worldview that might have laid the groundwork for our calamitous Kali Yuga? Something missing but essential to the lasting health of the Western psyche? Recall Socrates in conversation with his philosophic friends in prison just before his execution for promoting strange gods and being too clever for his democratic enemies.

Socrates was not known for writing anything, so the poet Evenos was curious about him turning a fable of Aesop into a lyric for a song. Socrates explained that he wasn't competing with anybody but responding to a dream with a message: "Socrates, make music—and work at it (*ergazou*)." Strange dream, but what could it possibly mean? Socrates was concerned. A little defensively, he said that he already practiced the greatest form of music, which, in his view, was the search for wisdom. Philosophy was Socrates's music.

But, about to imbibe the hemlock, to be on the safe side he tried in his awkward way to make some music. But the dream recurred and kept telling him to make music, as if there was something he had yet to acknowledge or to do. Perhaps there was more to the pursuit of wisdom than Socrates's logocentric art of conversation, which, we might say today, is only half of what our brain can deliver for us. We need music, painting, dance, all the arts and senses, all the modes of consciousness, right as well as left brain, soul along with intellect, all of it, if we hope to obtain something like wisdom.

Was there a more direct approach to higher consciousness, perhaps a different kind of wisdom, a more immediate mode of contact with the supreme energy and intelligence? Did Socrates miss the point of his dream when he reduced music to philosophy? Did he gloss over the difference between conceptual verbiage and ecstatic music? And there is an even more difficult question: Did he fail to consider the possibility of the rational part of the psyche tyrannizing, choking the life out of one's self or soul? Did he forget the danger of smothering the sensory and intuitive side of our mental life with ceaseless skeptical inquiry?

One of Plato's eighteenth-century admirers, the philosopher J. B. Vico, used the phrase "the barbarism of reflection" to describe the point in a society (or individual mind) where rules, reason, and rationality are used in such a way that the *sensus communis* is destroyed. At this stage of captious rationalism, basic shared values of humanity such as respect for truth, common decency and compassion, tolerance of difference, and good will for all are eroded, thus creating a Hobbsean mindset of war in which all is against all. Lost are the values that are the premise of any truly civil, no less progressive, society. Vico spoke of "that ultimate civil disease" in which people "have fallen into the custom of each man thinking of his own private interests . . . (and) in a deep solitude of spirit and will . . . they bristle and lash out at the slightest displeasure."[12]

Socrates's dream of music reveals doubts the philosopher might have had about his vocation in his last days. Rationality by itself may not be enough to bind together a society of diverse beings with diverse passions and personalities. Euripides's play, *The Bacchae,* is about a feminist revolt against the tyranny of state-imposed rationality. The ancient Greeks, whose creative contribution to world culture was extraordinary, were a people that apparently treasured ecstatic madness (*mania*). This is exhaustively demonstrated in a powerful study by Yulia Ustinova.[13]

In Plato's dialogue *Phaedrus,* Socrates lauds the value of *mania,* creative madness—in poetry, in prophecy, in healing, and in erotic love. However, it has to be a "god-inspired" form of madness; in particular, the god Dionysos. It must have been disconcerting for the more sober, even-tempered Greek establishment to face the arrival of the Thracian Dionysos and the cohorts of women inspired to join him in their nighttime bacchanalian mountain dances.

The Dionysian ethos inspired the tragic and the comic drama festivals. The comic genius and Dionysian spirit have this in common: they resonate with deep parts of our psyches that are disposed to upend "normal" reality, as we see in the comic plays of Aristophanes. Dionysian psychic reality and its ceremonial demands could be quite extreme and, at times, terrifying.

Imagine living in a small town somewhere in the United States and there's a knock on your door. You open the door and hear drums and enchanting flute riffs, and then a man with long hair and a beautiful epicene face, exuding erotic magnetism, appears. He's holding a thyrsus in his hand, which he strikes the ground with. Suddenly you hear the sounds of strange animals, and there's a panther under your cherry tree and an eagle poised on your chimney top.

It is the god of nature, Dionysos, who, with his retinue of drummers and flutists, is supernormally attractive, to women in particular. And so your wife, your mother, your daughter, possibly your sprightly grandma, are caught up by the magic vibe, drop everything, and follow Dionysos; they join the wild, sometimes destructive, dance, becoming what the Greeks called *maenads,* or madwomen. The arrival of Dionysos might well cause an upheaval.

In the ancient play, we witness the conflict between the shapeshifting Dionysos and a chief of the established order, Pentheus, who wanted to destroy the cult of the wild dancing god. Pentheus, the State rationalist, lost his battle against Dionysos, and in the end lost his life, undergoing *sparagmos,* the tearing apart of his body by the maenads who see him as desecrator of their divine music and of their sacred dance of liberation.

Moreover, in a howling turn of tragic irony he was torn to pieces by his mother, who was ecstatic with rage against the interloper and failed to see she was dismembering her own son. Euripides, through the voice of the Chorus, made the case for the Bacchae and against those who would repress the indestructible need of human nature to transcend itself by means of divine mania, also known as *ek-stasis*.

The *Bacchae,* an ancient Greek tragedy, is a defense of the rights of women and men to experience ecstasy (get out of themselves) and mania (escape one's state-defined identity). The deepest needs of the psyche must be satisfied within the bounds of civil society or else they will end by revolting against the established order. According to Greek tragedy playwright Euripides, there's a need for a space—call it sacred—that allows us to travel beyond our sober, self-contained everyday personas. Without some ceremonial concessions to the need for these extraordinary mental states, the return of the repressed will take revenge, as exemplified in the gruesome tale of Pentheus's mother dismembering her son.

Music and wild dancing phenomena recur in all shapes and forms throughout history. In the history of European Christianity, music in service to spiritual dance and ceremony has been a constant, periodically erupting into irrepressible movements. In many European dance epidemics, participants vied with the old Greeks in wildness, for example in the Festival of Fools, in which people donned costumes of animals, often disguising themselves as the other gender, happily doing and saying things out of character, all of which was outrageous to Christian piety.[14]

The "dancing" was not square or genteel but explosive, spastic, jerky, and hopping. There were dances meant to promote the fertility of crops, as well as of women, or to celebrate a saint or a holy day. The hungry, the sick, and the miserable danced for relief, for healing, for companionship. There were dances of the dead meant to help the dead but also to ward off the dangers that might issue from the insulted dead. J. G. Frazer, distinguished British folklorist and anthropologist, has documented the curious fact that early humanity lived in extreme fear of the dead, even dead folks who in life were friends and loved ones.[15] It's hard to avoid the impression that the intense ignorance of early peoples predisposed them toward a good deal of automatic paranoia.

Among the more evolved, many sang and danced at weddings and funerals, to join the angels in heaven and to repulse the devils from hell. Music and dance also appear as recurrently deployed instruments of release from the emotional woes and constraints of conventional life and established law. The majority of wild dancers tended to be women, no doubt desperate for periodic escape from patriarchal repression. Mania, as the old Greeks discovered, found a champion in the god Dionysos, who inspired women to go crazy and dance with divine abandon.

There is a strange side to music that is dark. You've probably heard of the Pied Piper of Hamelin. An odd little fellow comes strolling through town blowing tunes on his pipe and the children spontaneously break free and follow the Piper out of town and never come back. It's a true story, and 147 children were never seen again. All kinds of historical documentation bears this out. All we know is that the piping had the power to lure the children into whatever made them disappear.

As for the Dionysian frenzy, E. Lewis Backman, a professor of pharmacology from the University of Upsala, has tracked dance epidemics in Western history. An epidemic erupted in a region near the Rhine in 1374. That year was a time of unprecedented floods; the water of the Rhine was twenty-six feet higher than normal from the biggest snowfalls in hundreds of years. In the midst of this chaos arrived the choreomaniacs, victims of a mysterious disease called choreomania, dance mania, which became a big epidemic sweeping across Europe. According to one French historian, "the dancers were seized by some crazy madness, a frenzy hitherto unknown. They took off their clothes and went about naked; they put wreathes of flowers on their heads; they held each other hand in hand, and so they danced through the streets."[16] Was this a disease or a Dionysian explosion of ecstatic consciousness—an unconscious rebellion against boredom, poverty, and oppression? However bizarre and frightening their behavior, very few died; in the end, they all recovered and were restored to their normal selves.

ANOTHER APPROACH TO TRANSCENDENTAL MUSIC

In contrast to the Dionysian model of musical ecstasy, there is a gentler, though in the long run no less subversive, model of musical enlightenment we should consider. Little is known about Pythagoras, born in Samos around 560 BC. Famous for the theorem named after him, he is credited with discovering the mathematical scales and intervals of music, thus becoming a prophet of the union of science and spirituality. The laws and harmonies of music were taken to reflect the laws and harmonies of the *cosmos,* literally, the "ornament" of nature. Pythagoras conceived the idea of the "music of the spheres"—the inaudible structural harmonies of the cosmos. Pythagoras, I think, had a supernormal experience of music that inspired his amazingly bold idea of the music of the spheres. We will look at examples of this experience shortly.

It was the subtle sound of the mathematical harmonics of the universe that interested German astronomer Johannes Kepler, which led him to discover three basic laws of planetary motion, thus launching modern scientific astronomy. As the physicist Wolfgang Pauli wrote: "But these laws that Kepler discovered—the third after years of effort—are not what he was originally seeking. He was fascinated by the old Pythagorean idea of the music of the spheres (which, incidentally, played no small part of alchemy) and was trying to find in the movement of the planets the same proportions that appear in the harmonious sounds of tones and in the regular polyhedra.[17] Pauli and psychiatrist and psychoanalyst Carl Jung were concerned with how archetypal ideas and images can stimulate intuition and lead to objective scientific discoveries. Kepler was fascinated by the circle, the perfect geometric figure, but discovered that the planets did not move in circles but rather ellipses. Pauli wrote: "Circles were replaced by ellipses in 1609, a great revolution in astronomy!"

The connection between mathematics and music that Pythagoras found was understood to be a feature of the cosmos. This will come to suggest a paradigm of science that speaks to the beauty, resonance, and contemplative appeal of the natural world. From this music-tempered, Pythagorean perspective, science was structured as a way of life, a method of both uniting with and living in harmony with nature.

Iamblichus the Neoplatonist, in his *Life of Pythagoras,* paints a portrait of a man who was a mystic and a pure scientist. The unifying principle was called *amity:* "With respect to the amity which subsists in all things towards all, whether it be that of Gods toward men through piety and scientific theory, or of dogmas toward each other, or universally of the soul towards the body, and of the rational towards the irrational part through philosophy . . . or whether it be of men toward each other, of citizens indeed through sound legislation . . . or of husband to wife, or of brothers or kindred . . . or whether it be the pacification and the conciliation of the body which of itself is mortal, and of its latent contrary powers, through health, and a diet and temperance conformable to this." In a single word, we are told, it is "friendship" that best describes the hub of Pythagorean spiritual and scientific philosophy; a metaphysics of soul and music, a science of serenity that specializes in silence and secrecy.[18] This amity and friendship is built into the elements of nature, echoing the ontology of the natural world, of course, very unlike the four forces of the modern scientific worldview—gravity, electromagnetism, and strong and weak nuclear. Why indeed should the four known forces of physical nature be the only forces present and active in our world of experience? That would be sheer presumption. In fact, it's quite clear that we inhabit a whole world of forces: forces of a conscious, intentional nature and agents volitional, intuitive, affective, and attentive. So in the Pythagorean paradigm, the dominant principle is an inclination toward harmony among all sentient beings.

Scientists that might fit the Pythagorean paradigm today are the ecologists tracking the extinction of life forms, the pollution and over-heating of the planet, the habitat destruction, the plastic assault of the oceans, and all the rest. Today's Pythagoreans can't afford to be totally contemplative while the planet burns. The big question is, How shall we convert the climate crisis into a revolution of consciousness and a transformation of lifestyle?

Another class of unrecognized "scientists" of Pythagorean bent are indigenous peoples everywhere on Earth that, for thousands of years, learned how to adapt to their natural environments, enjoying and celebrating its wonders, however hard and demanding, without destroying them.[19]

The modern scientific paradigm of nature is the exact opposite of Pythagorean, for it is, by its nature, exploitative, destructive, and anthropocentric. Concern with beauty in any non-commerical sense sits at best in the back seat of mainstream science and technology. Much, if not most, of normal science and technology is practiced without moral, aesthetic, or social concern for Gaia; that is, for the air, earth, water, and once-teeming life forms of the planet.

An exercise of active imagination might be useful. My view on this is distinct from Jung's; in my view, psychokinesis (PK), mind over matter, is built into our psyches, liminal or subliminal, conscious or subconscious; it's always there as a permanent potential. The point about PK: it's very hard to predict when or how it will do its thing.

Animism is an enticing alternate worldview to entertain at this juncture of world history. Animism, which was the Greek philosopher Thales's dictum that all things are full of gods and souls, is viewed as the philosophy of the most primitive humans on Earth. And that may be just what is most needed. An animist is somebody who thinks and perceives everything as if it were alive: animated, sensitive, and responsive. So stars, rivers, mountains, sun, moon, land, sea, rain, sky, plant, and animal are all alive in subtle ways. If we change the way we perceive and think about Nature, we might learn to harmonize with Her. Imagine if we suddenly sensed everything around us breathing and faintly quivering with life.

Let's animate our imaginations and see our lakes and rivers as brothers and sisters; our seas and mountains as gods and goddesses; the breathing Earth in all its forms, the wondrous waters, the precious air, as alive with soul like us. More fully animated, we will sense and touch the spirit of life in all grades and forms of experience. Every experience will be an experiment; every experiment, a step toward self-transformation. The only requirement is to enter into dialogue with our deep mind, with whatever idea, dream, or fantasy tugs at our heart strings or haunts our night bed. The point is to make something of it: sing a tune you never sang before, write words that totally surprise you, dance a beautiful deed you never dared before.

The Pythagorean intuition of cosmic nature is symbolized by the monochord. "The monochord," wrote Joscelyn Godwin, a musician and scholar of mysticism, is "a one-stringed instrument used in musical pedagogy since antiquity that symbolizes the chain of being: the 'scale' of levels of existence that runs from the Earth to God."[20] The closer you get to God, the more beautiful the music, we are told. The monochord, in short, is a symbol of the cosmos.

But now to something truly extraordinary: music that breaks into our consciousness from the outer space of Pure Mystery. It simply involves being forcefully distracted from external reality, for example, while we're dreaming. We're forcefully pulled into sleep and dream nightly, and accounts of strange musical dreams go back to ancient history. Roman philosopher Cicero wrote that "in a dream, Scipio saw the heavenly firmament with its nine planetary orbits. . . . 'What is that sound, so loud and sweet, that fills my ears.' It is the sound which, connected at spaces which are unequal but rationally divided in a particular ratio, is caused by the vibration and motion of the spheres themselves, and, blending high notes with low, produces various harmonies; for such mighty motions cannot speed on their way in silence."[21] So in a special dream state, Scipio hears the "music of the spheres." Pythagoras claimed to have heard these transcendental sounds, but in a waking state.

Experiencing the music of the cosmos was the spiritual inspiration of Pythagorean philosophy. Pythagoras may have picked up his belief in reincarnation and respect for animal life on his travels to Egypt. He once reprimanded a friend for mistreating a dog. The philosopher claimed to know the person who had reincarnated in the dog. Eventually, his eccentric views on diet and animal liberation led to political problems in Samos.

So Pythagoras moved to Crotona, Italy, and founded a community of vegetarians that believed in animal liberation two and a half millennia before Peter Singer's brilliant study of animal rights and liberation.[22] The Pythagorean model of science will sound strange to modern ears; it was contemplative and committed to silence. Scientific knowledge was not meant to partner with economics, politics, or militarism. The enjoyment of knowledge for its own sake was the purpose of science, and was about living in harmony with one's community and natural environment. Pythagoras is quoted as saying that life was a festival: some come to compete in the games, some to sell their goods, and some (best of all, he says) to contemplate the beauty and harmony of the entire spectacle.[23] In this spirit, the "music of the spheres" is the consciousness of a fully animated perception of life, and may be heard and felt in places other than literal music.

Science and technology today don't celebrate the aesthetics or mysticism of life. The dominant paradigm serves the appetite for material goods, power, and boundless financial gain. The Pythagorean community was destroyed because of politics just as it probably would be today if (say) an American president were to mandate vegetarianism and the abolition of guns. The meat industries and gun lobbies would go after such a president with their meat cleavers and AR-15s.

In light of the dire 2021 U. N. report on climate change, the message is that we need to change the way we live on Earth. We need to learn how to use science and technology in ways that serve life as a whole, not the financial or ideological interests of small enclaves. A Pythagorean paradigm would buttress ecology and climate conservation. It would be a more "musical" model of science that embraced the whole of planetary life. Pauli has earned the moniker of "conscience of physics." He refused to join the team of scientists appointed to construct the first atom bomb that would be used on two Japanese cities, to kill forty thousand human beings in each *in one second*. In Pauli's view, science had no business aligning itself in any way with a technology of such inhuman destructive power. After the annihilations, physicists J. Robert Oppenheimer and Albert Einstein expressed their regrets. In contrast, Hungarian-American physicist Edward Teller was all in with the hydrogen bomb, which was thousands of times more destructive than the bombs dropped on Hiroshima and Nagasaki.

Pauli proved himself a true Pythagorean; today we know that the will to power over nature has caused Nature to respond with a catastrophic climate upheaval. The ill effects for all are growing exponentially; very soon, it will be *impossible* to deny the global catastrophic effects of the technological rape and abuse of our planet.

Pauli had a rich but troubling dream life that led him to consult with Jung, resulting in a mutually energizing twenty-year friendship. Pauli had difficulties with the kind of science that was evolving in the modern world, a grossly one-sided physicalism that ignored, if not invalidated, the psychical and mystical dimension of nature. He was therefore drawn to the Pythagorean paradigm based on exact science *and* the soulful practice of music, understood broadly to include all the arts and exploratory modalities of consciousness.

Pauli writes about Kepler who was a great figure on the threshold of a new scientific paradigm. The English physician Robert Fludd attacked Kepler for focusing too much on the quantitative side of planetary motion and neglecting the psycho-spiritual. Modern mainstream science automatically sides with Kepler and dismisses Fludd; Pauli does not. "I am for Kepler *and* Fludd," he writes, arguing for a more holistic paradigm of the scientific enterprise.

David Lindorff, a contemporary American reporter and filmmaker, summed it up this way: "Pauli believed that a point had been reached in which the mystical and the scientific should be rejoined as a complementary pair."[24] One might think here of the complementary particle-wave relationship, two sides of a larger, more complete reality. Pauli wrote: "It is the destiny of the occident continually to bring into connection with each other these two fundamental attitudes, on the one hand the rational-critical, which seeks to understand, and on the other the mystic-irrational, which looks for the redeeming experience of oneness."[25]

The call for a critique of the exclusivity of reductive materialism is alive today in many quarters. From the historical perspective, author Gregory Shaw's work on Neoplatonism and Iamblichus renders vivid the impoverishment of modern scientism: "Yet we have been denied the fullness of our heritage. The later Platonists were far more than speculative thinkers; they were also theurgists. They were adepts who had transcendent experiences and were perceived as divine men and women who possessed supernatural powers."[26] Pauli and Shaw (*et alia*) want to restore the psychic and spiritual dimension to the scientific venture; ecstasy, intuition, and imagination need to stand beside reason, analysis, and sensation. Science that ignores soul becomes science without soul.

MAGIC AND MUSIC
IN THE RENAISSANCE

In spite of physicalist science, and the un-mystical drift of modern humanity, the meme and the experience of transcendental music have persisted. We saw how the lure of the music of the spheres was linked through Kepler to the dawn of modern astronomy. We have also touched on music in the history of spontaneous dance movements and discussed the movements inspired by Dionysos, a god, and Pythagoras, a philosopher. We look now at how music figured in the medicine and philosophy of the fifteenth-century Renaissance in Italy. The magical and mystical uses of music during this period had to contend with the authority and dogmas of the Catholic church.

Two ways of making music were distinguished where psychical benefits might be obtained: the spiritual and the demonic. The latter marshals power by deploying witches, talismans, and substances unapproved by Catholic governance. Any extraordinary performance outside the church remit was construed as a threat to the power structure and therefore condemned as either inauthentic or diabolic.

A leading practitioner of Renaissance magic and medicine, Marsilio Ficino is regarded today as one of the founders of archetypal psychology.[27] Music was central to his philosophy of magic. The medium for creating music is of course air, *pneuma* in Greek, *spiritus* in Latin. Spiritus was cosmic and all-pervading. Music animates the air around us, creating soulpower out of air, which can be used for good (healing) or for ill (domination, seduction, etc.). The ill uses are akin to sorcery, which Ficino wisely backed off from. Interested in spiritual music, he relied on natural air, thus overcoming the dualism of mind and matter.

Attempting to explain why he combines musical and medical studies, Ficino wrote: ". . . since song and sound arise from the cogitation of the mind, the impetus of the phantasy, and the feeling of the heart, and, together with the air they have broken up and tempered, strike the aerial spirit of the hearer, which is the junction of the soul and body, they easily move the phantasy, affect the heart and penetrate into the deep recesses of the mind."[28]

Renaissance musicians used images and music to tune their psyches to the powers they believed were embedded in nature, and which they personified as gods, angels, spirits, and so on. It was thought possible to resonate with these archetypes and powers in ways that help us realize our selves and our creative endeavors. Nada Brahmananda did it when he focused without blinking on the murti of Shiva and drummed for thirty-five minutes on one breath. His theurgic aim was to identify with Shiva and therefore do something impossible. "I no Earth man," Nada kept cheerfully saying.

Ficino improvised music on his lyre;* it was meant to strengthen his spirit. In the *Book of Life,* he argues that sound is more powerful than sight, for it can move and stir the whole body to its core. And it can inspire the dance. He wrote, "Musical sound, more than anything else perceived by the senses, conveys, as if animated, the emotions and thoughts of the singer's or player's soul . . . it floods us with a wonderful pleasure; by its nature, both spiritual and material; it at once seizes, and claims as its own, people in their entirety."[29] In a related discussion of the Tantric philosophy of mind and body, which also avoided toxic dualism, religious studies researcher and professor Loriliai Biernacki wrote: "Thus, the goal is to let the sense of being object dissolve; what emerges as a consequence is a naturally inherent sense of subjectivity. In this case, the object itself, the body here, transforms from inert matter into consciousness and a body capable of extraordinary feats."[30]

Air, which surrounds and transcends us in space, is the medium of music; in music we are expanded in space, unbound from the body. The sound of music takes us into and out of our bodies, altering our sensations of space. The effects of verbal abstractions on our nervous system pale by comparison. Ficino believed it possible for us to consciously merge with the *spiritus mundi*—the cosmic spirit flowing through the whole of the sensible universe. Music, as Swami Nada said from the start, was essentially rhythm. But the idea of rhythm is not confined to music; it is found in the patterns of natural life, in all the arts, in all

---

*A superb CD of Ficino's prose and music, *Secrets of the Heavens* is available from Riverun Records.

forms of creativity. In painting, it's called composition; in poetry, it's prosody. Music, according to Ficino, is the most direct way of feeling the rhythmic life of the cosmic spirit.

Music is medicine for minds that feel the isolating effects of the Kali Yuga. During Ficino's Renaissance, imagination became the soul of religion, which was an active, creative process, not a rehash of stale theologies. The musical imagination would become the necessary healer.

Jung joined with the physicist Pauli in the quest for a new kind of science attuned to the archetypal healing wisdom of the soul. Science without soul unleashed an enemy of life that thinks of nature as a storehouse of raw materials to extract and deploy exclusively for human needs and financial gain.

Jung also inspired James Hillman, whose book *Re-Visioning Psychology* argued that the extraordinary creativity of the Renaissance occurred at times of appalling violence, danger, depression, and melancholy. "To imagine the Renaissance psyche," Hillman wrote, "we must enter a fantasy of street-knifings and poisonings, murder at High Mass, selling daughters, incest, torture, revenge, assassination, extortion, usury amid magnificence."[31]

Earlier, I said we *may* be on the threshold of a great renaissance of consciousness and lifestyle, but only because it may be the only way to manage the rapidly approaching climate upheavals that are already changing our lives. As if anticipating this back in the seventies, Hillman wrote: "It is as if we must go through a death experience in order to let go of our clutch on life. . . ." Indeed, research has shown that the near-death experience awakens an array of transformative forms of consciousness.[32] Hillman's psychology was about the liberation of soul and a process he called "soul-making" to help us see through the cultural devastations and falsifications of mainstream unselfconsciousness.

Hillman would have us personify the gods and spirits, which would help us confront and converse with them psychologically. Like William Blake, he believed that the gods reside within us in the form of archetypal images. He would have us de-literalize the images and forces that assail us and learn to engage with them in more imaginative ways. The point is to reimagine our beliefs and experience in ways that free us from the crushing weight of unwarranted assumptions. He argues for a polytheism of imagination to counteract the tyranny of monotheism of any type.

Hillman singles out Ficino, who was an impaired melancholic, as prime creator of a new paradigm of spiritual expressionism: "Renaissance Neoplatonism enabled the soul to welcome all its figures and forms, encouraging the individual to participate in the soul's teeming nature and to express soul in an unsurpassed outburst of cultural activity."[33] It was Ficino's translations of Plato, Plotinus, and Neoplatonist writers that laid the groundwork of this rebirth of the imaginative arts and sciences.

After dwelling on death as a major step in soul-making, we are reminded of the archetype that most gripped Ficino and Renaissance Italy. The "basic premise and concern was anima," Hillman wrote. The anima is the archetypal image of the feminine principle in the male psyche. When Romeo stationed himself under Juliet's balcony, the archetype was activated and charged with numinosity.

Hillman argued that the energies of Italy were animated by the feminine archetype to an extraordinary degree, and listed great figures of the time and the anima projections that inspired them. So, for example, Dante had Beatrice; Petrarch had Laura; Leonardo da Vinci had the Mona Lisa, which he carried around with him for thirteen years. The saints were animated by the imaginal figure of the Madonna, repeatedly painted, sculpted, and honored with song. The sight of a painting or statue of the Madonna would send Joseph of Copertino into the air with an unearthly scream. It was often observed that he remained aloft, raptured out of his senses, for hours.[34]

Hillman wondered: "I believe that were we better able to understand the psychology of the Renaissance, we might find both base and inspiration for a renaissance of psychology." The intense enlivening of the anima archetype during the Renaissance recalled the maenads and Dionysian dance ecstasy, central to the Greek creative genius that also caused fearful and repressive responses. Hillman mentioned two Renaissance achievements that spoke to the idea of the soul evolving: the invention of perspective in painting and the perfection of polyphonic music. The idea that our view of things is shaped by our particular perspective suggests that, by changing our perspective, we will see things differently. As for polyphony in the Renaissance, people who hear transcendental music also hear multitudes of voices in harmony.

State of mind is a crucial variable in this story, and the state we allude to as ecstasy is what makes this music transcendental. In Nietzsche's *Birth of Tragedy Out of the Spirit of Music,* he made the case for the polyphonic music of the Renaissance composer Palestrina, in contrast to opera, which he thought was tyrannized by words and concepts. The vaulted architecture of "the ineffably sublime and sacred music" of Palestrina is conducive to being "beside" oneself, *ek-static.* Transcendental music (or anything transcendental, I would say) takes us beyond the customary boundaries of our mundane mental life. Nietzsche distinguished emotion from ecstasy: emotion is always about me, good or bad; ecstasy is beyond me, and beyond good or bad. The young philosopher and Greek scholar made the case for ecstasy over the emotional life that inspires opera and its earthy, passionate music. Nietzsche, in fact, critiques the way the Western mind has been lulled into forgetfulness of entire realms of experience and modalities of consciousness. Nietzsche joins the ranks of Pauli, Hillman, and Jung in search of a scientific paradigm that enlarged the living sense of our higher life values.

SINGING FOR POWER

If Ficino was right and something like a cosmic spirit flows through our being—the Indians call it "kundalini energy"—we should expect it to break into consciousness from time to time. For this to happen, we need to be in a certain state of mind. Psychologist Kenneth Batcheldor concluded that absolute unwavering faith, trust, and confidence got results in his macro-PK experiments. Batcheldor trained groups of ordinary people to cause large physical objects to levitate without physically touching the object.[35]

If a person can arrange his or her consciousness in a way that rightly focuses on a particular goal, evidence shows that extraordinary things may happen. The advantage of a group setting is that nobody suffers from what's been called "ownership inhibition." It can be frightening to know that one person possesses such power; but in a group setting, the effect could not be laid at the feet of one person. Knowing that might let us turn off the brakes and unconsciously unleash our power.

We must fear the idea of strange experiences; there could be danger and a high price to pay. Hearing the strange songs of the Sirens can distract men at sea and lead them to their doom. Odysseus, however, was determined to listen to the song of the Sirens, but without risking any fatal mishap at sea; he ordered his men to stuff their ears with wax so they couldn't hear anything, then he instructed them to tie him to the mast of the ship. This way he was able to listen to the music of the Sirens, but without the risk of losing his head and behaving like a maenad.

Dangers aside, some indigenous societies have used the power of music in constructive ways, as in the following more recent example. In the early 1930s, the Humanities Council of Columbia University commissioned Ruth Murray Underhill to study the Indian Ceremonies of Southern Arizona.[36] The Papago tribe lived in a desert region of

Arizona on the boundaries of Mexico's sagebrush and lava rock mountains. They were a tribe that never fought against the European settlers and whom the Mexicans stayed away from; the parched terrain, almost without water, was forbidding and uninhabitable, so they were left alone. There was no way to capitalize on dominion of the land; the cost of bare survival would not be worth it. The natives, however, had adapted to their minimalist desert landscape.

What sort of people were the natives who built a unique culture from such meager natural resources, where water itself was always in short supply? We should pay attention because water shortage is becoming a major problem today as the planet gets hotter and dryer. Underhill's book paints a picture of the people and their most precious resource, the song magic the elders of the tribe used to cope with the basics of daily existence, be it food, or love, or war. There were songs for all aspects and circumstances of their lives.

The song magic, as practiced by the Papago, is a perfect fit for physicist Helmut Schmidt's model of how psychokinesis works. I'll get to that point shortly, but first I want to describe the character of the Papago, who spoke, in part, the language of their Aztec ancestors. The uniquely barren and unforgiving desert climate forced them to evolve in noticeably unique ways. Underhill cited three features of the people she studied and spent so much time with. "The Papagoes are a gentle, poetic branch of the race that produced the Aztec conquerors. Squat, broadfaced, dark, often with the beauty of a clean-featured piece of sculpture." First, they speak softly and never raise their voice, so it would be a boon if you could read lips. Second, the dead heat had slowed them down, so that every gesture is rhythmic, controlled, and conscious, with no trace of wasted effort—no casual or spontaneous gesticulations. Third, and most winsome, they seem constantly and naturally to be bubbling up with gentle laughter.

Adapting to unusually hard environmental constraints, they compensated in ways that enriched and humanized their culture. The

Papago are the perfect paradigm for us to contemplate, for we too have to adapt as creatively as we can, as we continue to be forced to cope with climate-induced constraints on how we live. The Papago used humor, music, and poetry to celebrate the joys and negotiate the challenges of their lean lifestyles. The song magic was key; they used it to shape, interpret, and direct their daily experience.

What do we mean by magical? There are many uses of the term, but the sense I intend has been scientifically elucidated in Dean Radin's book, *Real Magic*.[37] In plain language, the real thing refers to any instance of mental activity that directly influences, in some physical way, events in the physical world. Magic is the great short cut, bypassing the customary constraints of sense and brain, variously affecting the physical world. Radin made it clear that real magic is a power that is always potentially present in the world where there are conscious beings. Magic, or PK, is one of the latent potentials of intentional consciousness itself.

There is the common magic of our mind-body abilities such as using a spoon to stir a cup of coffee or playing a game of tennis or perhaps drawing a picture. These are so commonly observed they don't seem magical or miraculous. Nevertheless, there is a question—how indeed can a thought, a thing with no physical properties and no location in space, how could such a *no thing* activate my neuromuscular apparatus so I can stir my coffee? Between the magic of normal controlled movement and, say (to give a more dramatic illustration), the airborne movement of full-blown levitation, there are countless varieties and gradations of psychophysical so-called magic.

So now we can ask how Papago song magic works. According to Underhill, "The describing of a desired event in the magic of beautiful speech was to them the means by which to make that event take place. All their songs describe such desired events. . . . The songs are from every department of life and in many moods: solemn, wistful, humorous, wild." She added a crucial point: the song must be vivid, so you can see or feel it in detail. And it has to be sung in the right mood and manner for the real magic to manifest.

Real magic will not fly with your average materialist, but physicist Helmut Schmidt's PK experiments shed light on Papago song magic. He has performed PK experiments targeting events on the quantum level, and found that the PK worked in the same way that Papago song magic worked—*by concentrating on the outcome.*

In the experiment, a light display on a computer screen represents the hits and misses. The subject is asked to focus on the light display and try to make the light appear on the right or left side of the panel. The subject knows nothing of how the light display is connected to a random source of atomic decay. With no worries about how the quantum event and the light display or the computer work are connected, *you just focus on the result you're aiming for.* And there you have it— the essence of magic, the perfect fusion if intention and attention. The magic consists of a certain kind and degree of mental focus and the effects it produces. So we all have the basic equipment for making magic: our minds and the ability to direct our attention toward a goal. In essence, that's it. How far we go with our natural endowment is an open question.

A point about how the Papago songs are made: "Such a magic spell is never consciously composed." It is "given, by the supernatural powers."[38] The words of the song come to him as a "spontaneous uprush," to use F. W. H. Myers's phrase, in a dream or waking trance. It must be received, not constructed. And the song is understood as somehow a collective creation. Crucial is knowing how to wait for a dream or vision, the subliminal flash of insight. The spontaneous uprush has the effect of infusing faith and trust in the power of the poem. The power is available, but it needs to be named and evoked in the right way. But now to something distinctly and highly strange.

ENCOUNTERS WITH
TRANSCENDENTAL MUSIC

My lessons with Swami Nada made me think about the power and deep meaning of music. All good music can enrich our sense of the moment, but some experiences of music are more mysterious and sometimes transformative. Pythagoras claimed he heard "the music of the spheres," and used music as the ceremonial basis of his pacifist community of vegetarians and animal libertarians.

It may be rare, but there are modern reports of hearing the strange forms of music we're calling transcendental. Cases in the psychiatric literature of hallucinations may involve music, but they lack the transcendental features, including ecstatic joy, breathtaking beauty, marvelous aftereffects, and so forth. But there is a class of musical experience which is in no way pathological, it is best described as transpersonal and transcendental. The origin is obscure. The sounds seem to emerge softly from nowhere, linger a while, sometimes for a long while, rise to a crescendo, and then slowly fade away. The first person to collect and analyze reports of this phenomenon in the early twentieth century was the Italian psychical researcher, Ernesto Bozzano.

Bozzano identified several categories of the experience: music produced in the context of mediumship, cases associated with telepathy, and cases that involve hauntings and other events related to death and dying. For the first category, he reports the following— music heard around a particular person known to be a medium: "Mrs. Tamblin was the first medium through whom the guitar or other music instruments were played, without visible contact, so as to recognize specific tunes. In her presence it was played with all the exactness of an experienced musician, although she is not acquainted with music, or herself able to play any instrument. The tones varied from loud to vigorous to the most refined touches of the strings that could be imagined."[39]

Bozzano cites D. D. Home and W. S. Moses for their remarkable phenomena. Both were well-known mediums, and Home especially was investigated by leading scientists of the day such as Sir William Crookes. In his autobiography, Home wrote about what happened to him in Boston, apparently having "the most impressive manifestations of music without any earthly instruments. At night, when I was asleep, my room would be filled as it were with sounds of harmony, and these gradually grew louder until other persons in other parts of the house could hear them distinctly."[40] So it is clear that some of the incidents are clearly public and therefore in some sense objective.

In July, 1868, Lord Adare wrote: "Almost immediately after we had gone to bed and put the lights out, we both heard the music . . . but more powerful and distinct. Home said the music formed words, that it was a voice speaking and not instrumental music. I could hear nothing but chords like an organ or harmonium played at a distance."[41] The same psychic phenomenon is interpreted or perceived differently. Even in normal types of experience, the same event often generates divergent perceptions and interpretations.

A more reserved medium, Stainton Moses was a person around whom others also heard strains of unexplained music. In 1893, a Mrs. Speer published the following description of her experience of transcendental music: "Before meeting this evening we heard fairy bells ringing in different parts of the garden where we were walking. At times they sounded far off, seemingly playing at the top of some high elm trees, music and stars mingling together; then they would approach nearer to us, evidently following us into the séance room which opened on to the lawn."[42]

In both of these examples, more than one person reports hearing music, suggesting the objectivity of these occurrences. At the same time, individuals often report hearing differences; as we saw, some hear words while others nearby will just hear the sounds of music, without the words. The effect of awe and wonderment is usually the same. Many reports say that the music is heard in crescendo, starting in a whisper and gradually getting louder, peaking in power, perhaps moving around in space, and then, in reverse, becoming less audible and gradually returning to silence.

In Bozzano's second category, the mysterious music became the sign of a telepathic connection, as in this case of a woman and her dead husband, both musicians. The woman's child was resting on her lap as she sat in a rocking chair. An older daughter, in their otherwise empty house, recounted what then happened: "Suddenly, we begin to hear celestial music, with a sad modulation but very sweet, which continues all around us for two minutes, which then gradually fades away into silence." During the music, the mother reportedly slipped into ecstatic rapport with her deceased husband, and as she did, the ten-year-old James jumped from his mother's lap and cried out, "Father! Father!" and ran toward the spot where his father usually sat at his piano.[43] The unexplained music was heard at the moment of a telepathic connection between mother, deceased father, and son. And so it seems that a curtain was temporarily drawn, a moment of harmony between souls on the earthly side of the great divide and a soul presumably on the other side.

The next two categories of the phenomenon are closely related. Shades of such mysterious music are reported in the context of hauntings and generally near, at, or after somebody's death. There seems a variety of ways and contexts in which this music is heard. My hunch is that the transcendental world and source of the mysterious music is present to us all the time, but muted in the subliminal depths of our mental life, buried under the blanket of our normally cluttered and distracted lives. Every now and then, however, inlets to some of our psychic potentials suddenly open up and things happen that we call strange, paranormal, or miraculous.

We have clues to how the various inlets to the greater consciousness open up. Everything depends on the vector of our everyday intentions.

Most of us are absorbed in, if not totally identified with, our precarious bodily, social, and economic struggles. And all this on an overheated planet facing more and more violent hurricanes, tornadoes, floods, droughts, starvation, toxification, pollution, water wars, cyber warfare, crazy conspiracy theories, and so forth. Amid all this noise, who has ears for transcendental music? There is much competition for our consciousness during the twilight of the Kali Yuga. It's hard to focus on inner realities when the world around us is falling apart.

And yet, even amid the storm and stress of life, breakthroughs of consciousness are taking place somewhere, unexpected and unpredicted. People experience music of a sort that takes them beyond themselves, causing them to feel as if they are vibrating in unison with the heart of humanity and the soul of the universe. It can happen to anybody in almost any circumstance, but especially in experiences that shake up the link between mind and body. During dissociated states, in the gap of mental space that opens, we're more porous to external influence. Moreover, the more severe the disruption, the larger the gap that allows the glimpse or sound or whatever form the breakthrough assumes.

Bozzano and musician and psychical researcher Scott Rogo found that many who heard what seemed to qualify as transcendental music had some form of out-of-body experience, or else, even more disruptive, were in some way closer than usual to bodily death. So we land in a paradox that links the thing we fear most, death, with transcendent music, joy, and spiritual transformation. It almost seems like a surrealist joke, a masterpiece of incongruous juxtaposition.

Rogo was an avid hunter of anomalies, especially lawbreakers of materialism. In his two books on nad (nada; he omits the *a*), he collected, from various sources, documented accounts of unexplained experiences of music. For instance, a Mrs. E. Hatfield described how a drug accidentally triggered her experience. "In 1927, I was given ether. I seemed to float down a dark tunnel, moving toward a half-moon of light that was miles away. I heard the sound of music and smelled the scent of an old-fashioned bouquet." But then she heard a voice telling her to go back to life, a command she resisted, but couldn't for long and found herself back in her body. "I am convinced that I was dead to this world but wholly alive in another," she wrote.[44] Again, we obtain the impression of being poised right on the edge of another world, another dimension of reality. A hit of ether instantly triggers a memorable metaphysical adventure.

Illness can precipitate these sudden transcendental leaps. A girl of sixteen years was in bed, ill, and began to feel woozy, but then: "Suddenly I realized a feeling of great excitement, wonder, and delight surpassing anything I had ever experienced as I felt my body weightless and floating upwards in a golden glow towards a wonderful light around hazy welcoming figures *and the whole air was filled with beautiful singing.*"*[45] The experience became an icon, perhaps a lodestar, for this girl as she evolved into her forties, according to her account. Once again, the experience came suddenly and briefly, in the uneasy sleep of an illness, just enough to set the curtain aside for a glimpse and audition of another reality.

A case reported in the "Proceedings of English Psychical Research" is about a perfectly healthy Mr. Skelton spontaneously having this experience: "I was engaged with two other men one day about two o'clock p.m. in taking out some evergreen trees from a boxcar to take home and set out; they were large and heavy—just at that instant I saw a medium-sized person standing at my right hand, clothed in white with a bright countenance." This sudden companion led the narrator into a world of transcendent light where he met all his deceased friends and relatives. He stated, "I saw many thousand spirits clothed in white, and singing heavenly music—the sweetest song I ever heard."[46] What is remarkable was the utterly smooth, unexpected and unintended way

---

*Italics mine, added for emphasis.

he slipped from moving some evergreen trees with his friends on Earth into another world of light, music, and visions of deceased loved ones. The move was no more difficult than opening one's eyes from being asleep. William Blake once said that death was just like stepping from one room to another. How convenient!

In a case reported by Catherine Crowe in her remarkable book *The Night Side of Nature*, we learn of an unusual haunting and poltergeist; many witnesses were involved who heard physically unexplained music. "One of the most remarkable features in this case is the beautiful music which was heard by all the parties including the unbelieving father. . . . This music was heard repeatedly during a space of sixteen weeks; sometimes it was like an organ, but more beautiful; there was singing of holy songs, the words being distinctly heard."[47] All this pointed to some kind of strange reality, which revolved around a twelve-year-old girl, Mary Jobson, who was seriously ill but recovered. Notably, the music continued to be heard after Mary got well, for sixteen weeks. Just being in the vicinity of possible death may open the inner ear of some people, in some contexts, and give them a prolonged hearing of Swami Nada's *unstruck* otherworldly sound. In this case, *unstruck* becomes a synonym for *origin unknown*. Sixteen weeks of transcendental music is the longest run of the phenomenon I've come across.

Facts suggest there are many ways our inner ears may be opened to these anomalous auditions. What seems clear: a certain kind of altered state of consciousness enables the sudden influx—for example, illness, mediumship, hauntings, and spontaneous out-of-body experiences. In addition, we have reports of saints, yogis, and contemplatives also claiming to have had such experiences.

Rogo gave several examples of clairaudient Catholic mystics. St. Therese de Lisieux (1873–1897) lived a short life of twenty-four years. What she said about music just before she died will serve as her poetic epitaph: "Mother, some notes from a distant concert have just reached my ears, and the thought came to me that soon I shall be listening to the music of Paradise." The English St. Chad died in 671, a victim of the plague. A week before his death music was heard around him by others. Notice that here the strange intrusion is precognitive. Owen, a person listening in the garden, threw up his hands in astonishment while listening, and Chad said: "That is the angels who are singing; in seven days they will come back to fetch my soul."[48] And, a week later, he was dead.

Rogo referred to Domenico Bernini's biography of St. Joseph of Copertino (1603–1663)—a perfect illustration of the view that the more one gets detached from everyday reality, the greater the likelihood of falling into an altered state conducive to transcendental experience. St. Joseph's life and behavior embodied the very archetype of unworldliness. If you can imagine Joseph's lifestyle universalized, the same day would be the end of war and corporate capitalism. Life on Earth would be totally different. It's hard not to be a little amused by the saint's super sensitivity. Joseph displayed signs of a panic attack when a humble female devotee once offered him a new under-garment as a gift. He acted as if to accept new underwear would imply a deep restructuring of his existence, devoted to willing his whole being and total consciousness on Heaven, the Madonna—the great *beyond*. Joseph was very good at divorcing himself from established reality. He saw a bit of underwear from a female as something that could throw him into ungodly disarray. Joseph and Nada were alike in their single-minded aspiration to make a clean sweep of every possible distraction from their one transcendent goal—union with the supreme, with the Divine.

Joseph's psychic detachment from reality was symbolically expressed by his spectacular disposition to levitate. The archives contain 150 sworn statements describing the saint's various gravity-defying performances. As for telepathy, he was so gifted in the mind-reading department that his superiors ordered him to desist from displaying it so readily. The annoying saint could catch you when your mind wandered from your prayers toward more mundane matters.

Music was more important to Joseph than preaching. He wrote lyrics and liked to sing his sacred rhymes in a style that resembled today's rap. His death was a phenomenon, carefully observed and recorded by his monastic brethren. Entirely original, his last and final days present us with the picture of a sixty-year-old man, giddy with joy, who can't wait to shake loose from his ailing body and die.

The surgeon Francesco di Pierpaolo deposed: "During his last illness, I was in the act of cauterizing his right leg . . . and I noticed that Padre Giuseppe was rising up into the air about a palm's length from the chair. . . . I got on my knees to better observe Padre Giuseppe, as did the doctor who was also present, and we both verified that not only was he entirely out of his senses but was floating above the ground in the air."[49]

Listening to music often triggered Joseph's levitations. The surgeon continued: "While I was in the room with the friar a few days before he died, Baccelliere Bonfini performed a beautiful rendition of the hymn, Ave Maria Stella. Padre Giuseppe fell into ecstasy" and remained in that state until the song ended.

Bernini described the moment of his death: "He asked for Extreme Unction, and showed as it was being performed, a force superior to the weakness caused by his illness . . . he began to speak in a strong voice: 'Oh those songs! Oh that sound of Paradise! Oh that smell! That taste! That fragrance! Oh that sweetness of paradise!'"[50] It is hard to avoid noting the multisensory heightening of Joseph's experience at the moment of his death, a phenomenon that seems like a total inversion of what common sense and materialist science would predict.

I don't want to end here leaving the impression that these experiences occur only to a few saints or yogis. Not at all; their occurrence is totally unpredictable and may occur to anybody.

CONCLUDING COMMENTS

Nada Brahmananda was at first a reluctant sannyasi, a man born to make music who wanted nothing else from life. Once a professor of music at a prestigious university, and for a while the court musician of the King of Mysore, he lost both these positions. Nearly driven to suicide as a result, he was finally roped into becoming a monk, his only refuge from the ravages of having to survive in worldly society. It was the only move he could make to preserve his sanity and do the thing he loved most. The result was to combine his musical talent with his spiritual life and, in this way, create his own unique identity. Jung would see a wonderful example of individuation, the art of harmonizing the various, sometimes conflicted, parts of ourselves, into a unified vibrant whole.

Nada has something to say to our tottering health care paradigm. He himself couldn't be dragged to a doctor, and he repeatedly said it made no difference to him whether he lived or died. Not exactly the best advice for the average human being, needless to say. This was a man who refused to even think of his health in conventional terms, although he was very careful about what he ate, and knew how to dodge traffic in midtown Manhattan. As far as I know, he never or rarely got ill and he died at the age of ninety-seven. Nada embodied his own health care paradigm, which involved extraordinary breath control and the ability to generate different kinds of vibrations and direct them thoughtfully to all parts of his body.

This control over his body may explain his health and energy, sleeping just two hours a night and never dreaming—a subject worthy of further inquiry. But from Nada we get a powerful reminder that we need an ally in this dangerous life, and the Indians have a word for it: sadhana, spiritual practice. This can be almost anything that activates our mental life, any practice that forces us to try, test, persist, invent, risk, endure, and enjoy our efforts toward self-mastery. Sadhana is practice geared toward transcendence, however that pans out. The sadhana we embrace has to resonate with us, allowing our peculiar talents and dispositions to find their way. For one person it will be prayer and meditation, another sport, another the arts or the helping professions, or anything you invent *de novo* and make work for yourself. Needed is a practice that puts us in touch with our soul life, respects our passion, and fires our imagination.

Now there's the unavoidable question about coping with the Kali Yuga—the cultural and political wars, multiplying weather disasters, and horrific economic disparity everywhere. We look around today and see sudden, unexpected loss and destruction in all quarters. Nada Brahmananda saw the world as a great dream, "on film," he would say, an illusion, compared to the extrasensory spiritual world within and beyond us. However grim the immediate outlook of the present world, in my opinion, Nada's life was an authentic witness to a transcendental dimension. At the same time, I'm forced to observe that the dominant culture seems in large part to have lost contact with this transcendental dimension.

The need for a new paradigm of science is increasingly felt by people everywhere, whatever words or slogans are used. Pauli's idea of a Pythagorean paradigm has been a motif, a meme of the imagination throughout history, an archetype for folks distressed by how science and technology made possible the permanent threat of nuclear annihilation and a global climate crisis that threatens to destroy world civilization.

Pythagoras had a musical, meditative view of science and mathematics. His over-arching metaphysical principle was amity, and the communities that followed him understood science as a means to peace and the liberation of all life forms—the exact opposite of how most science and technology operate today. In the Pythagorean paradigm, scientific knowledge is about living in accord with nature. Forms of nature like rivers and trees and mountains are sacred, and may not be desecrated by the gross profiteering instinct. Pythagoras believed in animal rights because he believed that animals have feelings; we should therefore treat them with kindness, especially since the dog you beat today might be an old friend or one of your revenant uncles.

Pythagoras believed in reincarnation; some of us are likely to come back as animals, especially dogs and horses, or, quite possibly, as one of Nada's despised pigs. The Pythagorean paradigm would be bad news for the meat industries. It would bode ill for consumerism, in general. It would certainly be the end of the arms industries. The trillions of dollars the corporations usually get would stay with the people and be used to educate and enhance their lives. An archetype needs to come to life in which science would embrace soul, mind, heart, and consciousness. In this life-centered paradigm, creating weapons of mass murder and worshipping the profit motive would be anathema.

Everything about the world we have constructed tends to deafen us to the more subtle music and harmonies of life and death. And yet wherever there is experience, the artist within us may discover the healing music in the rough sounds of ordinary life. The creative imagination isn't some occasional add-on to life but is the soul of our everyday perceptions and activities. Every moment of experience presents us with a field of options, different ways of seeing what is before us, making it trivial or beautiful, meaningless or momentous. No matter the contingency, if we draw on the powers within, we're free to shape the tone, the color, the meaning of our day-to-day experience. The facts are one thing; how we integrate the facts is another.

At any moment, there are two ways to experience the world; in one we're passive, conservative, content with the familiar, averse to novelty, frightened by the unknown, inclined to rigidity, preoccupied with safety, obsessed with boundaries, and so on. In the other, call it the creative way, we're active and mobile, receptive to novelty, friendly to the unexpected, open to the astonishing, fearless, and compassionate.

Everybody has a story and everybody has an unconscious artist trying to make music in a world of noise that would drown them out. Music, in this universal sense, is the pattern of soul that we fashion out of what life and chance give us to work with. A single note can create a portal to transcendence, while the wrong note can trap us in the dumps of the soul. Nada Brahmananda invites us to make music out of our lives. Do it now, and don't be afraid to improvise. All you need, he said, is a sense of rhythm, a listening ear, and a heart that throbs. Keep practicing the music of your life and, to quote the singing Swami, you will "come correct."

Notes

PREFACE

1. Plato, *Plato's Phaedo* (Oxford:Clarendon Press, 1911).

I. LAUGHING MASTER FROM A DREAM

1. Wallace Stephens, "Peter Quince at the Clavier." Available online at Poetry Foundation.

8. A GIFT FROM AN OLD MAN

1. Erlendur Haraldsson, *Miracles Are My Calling Cards: On the Psychic Phenomena of Sathya Sai Baba* (London: Century, 1987).

21. REFLECTIONS ON TRANSCENDENTAL MUSIC

1. Michael Grosso, *The Man Who Could Fly* (Lanham, Md.: Rowman & Littlefield, 2016).
2. See William Howitt, *The History of the Supernatural in All Ages and Nations* (Cambridge, UK: Cambridge University Press, 1863/2010).
3. See John M. Watkins, *Orpheus* (London, 1965).
4. James Hillman, *Re-Visioning Psychology* (New York: Harper Colophon, 1975).
5. Michael Grosso, *Smile of the Universe: Miracles in an Age of Disbelief* (Charlottesville, Va.: Anomalist Books, 2020).

6. Alfonso Caycedo, *India of Yogis* (New Delhi: Caxton Press, 1966).

7. Annekatrin Puhle, *Light Changes: Experiences in the Presence of Transforming Light* (Hove: White Crow Books, 2013).

8. Grosso, *Man Who Could Fly.*

9. Alain Daniélou, *Music and the Power of Sound* (Rochester, Vt.: Inner Traditions, 1995).

10. Edward Kelly and Ian Whicher, "Patanjali's Yoga Sutra and Siddhis," in *Beyond Physicalism,* ed. Edward Kelley (Lanham, Maryland: Rowman & Littlefield, 2015), 315–348.

11. Alain Daniélou, *While the Gods Play: Shaiva Oracles and Predictions on the Cycles of History and the Destiny of Mankind* (Rochester, Vt.: Inner Traditions, 1987), 36.

12. Giambattista Vico, *The New Science* (New York: Anchor Books/Knopf Doubleday, 1744), 381.

13. Yulia Ustinova, *Divine Mania: Alteration of Consciousness in Ancient Greece* (Milton Park, England: Rutledge, 2018).

14. E. Louis Backman, *Religious Dances* (London: Allen & Unwin, 1952).

15. James G. Frazer, *The Belief in Immortality and the Worship of the Dead* (London: Macmillan, 1913).

16. Backman, *Religious Dances,* 215.

17. David Lindorff, *Pauli and Jung: The Meeting of Two Great Minds* (Wheaton, Il.: Quest Books, 2004), 156.

18. Christopher Bamford, *Lindisfarne Letter: Homage to Pythagoras* (Lindisfarne, England: Lindisfarne Press, 1982), 27.

19. See Intergovernmental Panel on Climate Change (IPCC) website, 2021.

20. Joscelyn Godwin, *Harmonies of Heaven and Earth: Mysticism in Music* (Rochester, Vt.: Inner Traditions International, 1987).

21. Alexander Roob, *Alchemy and Mysticism* (New York: Taschen, 1997), 89.

22. Peter Singer, *Animal Liberation: A New Ethics for Our Treatment of Animals* (New York: Avon Books, 1975).

23. G. S. Kirk, J. E. Raven, and M. Schofield, *The Presocratic Philosophers* (Cambridge, United Kingdom: Cambridge University Press, 1957), 228.

24. Lindorff, *Pauli and Jung,* 92.

25. Lindorff, *Pauli and Jung,* 92.

26. Gregory Shaw, "Platonic Siddhas: Supernatural Philosophers of Neoplatonism," in *Beyond Physicalism* (Lanham, Md.: Roman & Littlefield Publishers, 2015), 275–313.

27. Hillman, *Re-Visioning Psychology.*

28. D. P. Walker, *Spiritual and Demonic Magic: From Ficino to Campanella* (University Park, Pa.: Penn State University Press, 2003), 6.

29. Walker, *Spiritual and Demonic Magic,* 9.

30. Loriliai Biernacki, "Conscious Body: Mind and Body in Abhinavagupta's Tantra," in *Beyond Physicalism* (Lanham, Md.: Roman & Littlefield Publishers, 2015), 349–386.

31. Hillman, *Re-Visioning Psychology,* 204.

32. Pim van Lommel, *Consciousness Beyond Life: The Science of the Near-Death Experience* (New York: Harper One, 2010).

33. Hillman, *Re-Visioning Psychology,* 200.

34. Grosso, *Man Who Could Fly.*

35. Kenneth James Batcheldor, "Report on a case of table levitation and associated phenomena," *Journal of SPR* 43 (1965): 339–356.

36. Ruth Murray Underhill, *Singing for Power: The Song Magic of the Papago Indians* (New York: Ballantine Books, 1973).

37. Dean Radin, *Real Magic: Ancient Wisdom, Modern Science, and a Guide to the Secret Power of the Universe* (New York: Harmony Books, 2018).

38. Underhill, *Singing for Power.*

39. Ernesto Bozzano, *Phenomenes Psychiques Au Moment de la Mort* (Paris: Temps Present, 1923), 180–255.

40. D. Scott Rogo, *Nad: A Study of Some Unusual "Otherworld" Experiences* (New York: University Books, 1970), 94–95.

41. Rogo, *Nad,* 94.

42. Rogo, *Nad,* 96.

43. Rogo, *Nad,* 92–94.

44. Rogo, *Nad.*

45. Alistair Conwell, *The Audible Life Stream: Ancient Secret of Dying While Living* (Winchester: John Hunt Publishing, 2015), 122.

46. Rogo, *Nad.*

47. Rogo, *Nad,* 74–75.

48. Omer Englebert, *The Lives of the Saints* (New York: Barnes & Noble Books, 1994), 85.

49. Michael Grosso, *Wings of Ecstasy: Domenico Bernini's Vita of St. Joseph of Copertino* (N.p.: CreateSpace, 2017), 124.

50. Grosso, *Wings of Ecstasy,* 124.

Recommended Reading

Daniélou, Alain. *Northern Indian Music*: *Theory & Technique*. (Vol. One) London: Christopher Johnson, 1949.

———. *Music and the Power of Sound*: *The Influence of Tuning and Interval on Consciousness*. Rochester, Vt: Inner Traditions.

———. *The Ragas of Northern Indian Music*. New Delhi: Munshiram Manoharlal Publishers Pvt. Ltd, 2014.

Godwin, Joscelyn. *Harmonies of Heaven and Earth: Mysticism in Music*. Rochester, Vt: Inner Traditions, 1994.

Iamblicus. *The Life of Pythagoras*. MSAC Philosophy Group, 2008.

Lindorff, David. *Pauli and Jung: The Meeting of Two Great Minds*. Wheaton, Il: Quest Books, 2004.

Macchioro, Vittorio. *From Orpheus to Paul: A History of Orphism*. New York: Henry Holt, 1930.

Rogo, D. Scott. *Nad: A Study of Some Unusual "Other-World" Experiences*. New York: University Books, 1970.

———. *Nad, Vol. II, A Study of "The Music of the Spheres."* Secaucus, NJ: University Books, 1972.

Russolo, Luigi. *The Art of Noises*. New York: Pendragon Press, 1986.

Sacks, Oliver. *Musicophilia: Tales of Music and the Brain*. New York: A.A. Knopf, 2007.

BOOKS OF RELATED INTEREST

Chakra Frequencies
Tantra of Sound
by Jonathan Goldman and Andi Goldman

Healing Sounds
The Power of Harmonics
by Jonathan Goldman

Tuning the Human Biofield
Healing with Vibrational Sound Therapy
by Eileen Day McKusick

Awakening the Chakras
The Seven Energy Centers in Your Daily Life
by Victor Daniels, Kooch N. Daniels, and Pieter Weltevrede
Illustrated by Pieter Weltevrede

Vibrational Medicine
The #1 Handbook of Subtle-Energy Therapies
by Richard Gerber, M.D.

The Power of Sound
How to Be Healthy and Productive Using Music and Sound
by Joshua Leeds

Seed Sounds for Tuning the Chakras
Vowels, Consonants, and Syllables for Spiritual Transformation
by James D'Angelo, Ph.D.

The Six Healing Sounds
Taoist Techniques for Balancing Chi
by Mantak Chia

INNER TRADITIONS • BEAR & COMPANY
P.O. Box 388 • Rochester, VT 05767
1-800-246-8648 • www.InnerTraditions.com

Or contact your local bookseller